LA *by* MOUTH

THE ESSENTIAL GUIDE
TO EATING IN LOS ANGELES

MIKE POSTALAKIS

The Countryman Press
A division of W. W. Norton & Company
Independent Publishers Since 1923

Image on pages 1, 7, 198, and 204: © Booblgum/iStockphoto.com
Image on pages 19, 57, 97, 119, 159, and 181: © art_of_sun/Shutterstock.com

For information about permission to reproduce selections from this book,
write to Permissions, The Countryman Press, 500 Fifth Avenue,
New York, NY 10110

For information about special discounts for bulk purchases, please contact
W. W. Norton Special Sales at specialsales@wwnorton.com or 800-233-4830

Manufacturing by Versa Press
Book design by Lidija Tomas
Production manager: Devon Zahn

The Countryman Press
www.countrymanpress.com

A division of W. W. Norton & Company, Inc.
500 Fifth Avenue, New York, NY 10110
www.wwnorton.com

978-1-68268-192-3 (pbk.)

10 9 8 7 6 5 4 3 2 1

For Mom,
who still makes
the best spaghetti.

CONTENTS

Guerrilla Tacos

INTRODUCTION

"The primary requisite for writing well about food is a good appetite."

—A. J. Liebling

Los Angeles by Mouth is about the experience of dining out in Los Angeles, written from the perspective of a person who very much likes dining out in Los Angeles, and has been doing so for years now. By no means do I claim to be an expert in the culinary arts, but I'm an adventurous, endlessly curious and discriminating food lover, obsessed with the vitality and eclecticism of the prospering Los Angeles restaurant scene—though in Los Angeles, as you'll see, the word "restaurant" has taken on a certain elasticity to encompass the variety of venues at which you can sample the finest provender on offer: food trucks, pop-up restaurants, French dip joints, tree houses . . . the list of food-purveying venues goes on. Although tree houses are not actually a thing. Yet.

Think of this as an informed enthusiast's guide rather than a compendium of snobbish judgments handed down from on high by a jaded pro who hasn't paid for a meal since college. Much like Nabokov, I have strong opinions, and I love sharing those opinions. But they're still just opinions. My advice would be to use this book as a kind of explorer's guide—a starting point for adventurous eaters to develop their own opinions. It's possible that you may disagree with one or two of my assessments. You'll be wrong, but that is your right as an American, or at least is at the time of writing. (I'm taking nothing for granted.)

There are a couple things you need to know about the food scene in LA. By "food scene" I mean something roughly analogous to "music scene," in the sense that the music scene in LA went through a really bad and prolonged hair metal slump in the late '80s but has since rebounded to produce a dizzying number and variety of good bands, most of which

Jon & Vinny's

moved to LA from Brooklyn to take advantage of the low rent. The same thing happened to the food scene! For a while—through the '80s and '90s and even the early aughts—most foodies thought of LA, if they thought of LA, as a wasteland populated by once-adventurous but now rote and uninspired fusion restaurants. Much like the over-simplified history I just presented of the Hollywood music scene, that was never actually true. LA has always had its culinary treasures. The difference now is that, well, there are a lot more of them, and people are starting to pay attention.

I was queuing for food trucks before it was cool to queue for food trucks, so I like to think that my length and breadth of experience exploring the many facets of Tinseltown gastronomy gives me an edge when it comes to guiding newbies to the cornucopia of delights that await in unexpected places, whether you're visiting or have just moved here, or have lived here for twenty years and don't go anywhere more wild and crazy than Canter's. Not to knock Canter's—it's one of my favorites, and it's open 24 hours, a rarity in Los Angeles—but there are other places to go.

A typical scene: I stand, by myself, in the nearly empty Vons parking lot on the north end of Alvarado Street, waiting patiently for the Taco Zone truck (technically a trailer) to open up.

From my vantage point, I can see a murderer's row of different meats simmering on the grill. When these have reached tender perfection, one of the cooks will grab a spatula and separate the meats into different metal containers.

I'm here thirty minutes early because it's Friday night and I have no plans, except to enjoy an *al pastor* burrito for dinner. Why so early? Because once the order window swings open and the scent of cooked

71 Above

meat wafts through Echo Park, an enormous, snaking line of human mouths with stylishly dressed bodies attached will form. I hate waiting in lines. But waiting in line before the line *starts* is totally cool.

By the way, when I say this burrito is for dinner—that's not entirely true. In fact, I've already had dinner. Three hours ago, high above the city in a swanky restaurant situated at the top of the tallest building in LA. The meal was great. I left completely satisfied. You'll read about it later in this very book. Nevertheless, even before I finished my meal, I had this burrito on my mind.

For those keeping score at home, in a roughly six-hour span I will have dined at a posh eatery where the chefs wear those big white hats, a food truck where hipsters congregate to devour tacos, and, finally, several hours later, I will plunk my butt in the booth of a diner that's been serving grilled cheese and onion rings (and pie!) since before your parents started dating.

That, dear reader, is dining in LA.

Los Angeles is a city of spectacular diversity. For the last hundred-plus years, people from all walks of life, including more than a few

Birdies

paperweight manufacturers and balloon artists, at some point in their lives heard the call "Go West," and listened to that call, and acted upon that call, and headed west with hopes of finding fame and fortune, or a psychiatrist who could help them stop hearing voices. First came the gold rushers, panning for days in raging rivers, talking to each other in funny, high-pitched crazy voices, according to a movie I saw. Then came those lured by the siren call of the silver screen; in the seventies, Laurel Canyon drew the longhairs—musicians, aspiring drug addicts, often both, who spent their days strumming a six-string and takin' it easy. Recent years brought the Revenge of the Nerds, responsible for the tech boom, which helped create the Segway, skateboards that explode, and the magical word machine with which I'm writing this book.

Nowadays the City of Angels has proven irresistible to a new

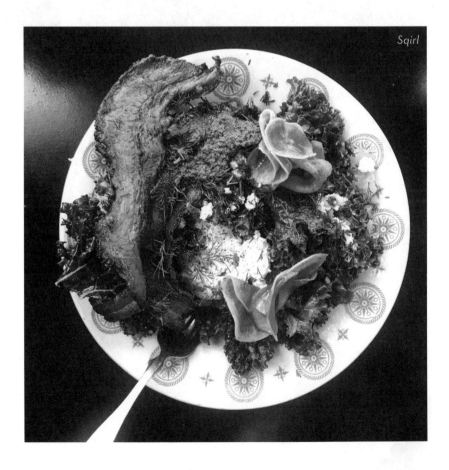

Sqirl

A.O.C.

generation of bold, daring, zeitgeist-attuned chefs. And my belly is all
the better (and bigger) for it!

But there's a lot more to this city than the new generation of chefs.
LA has a rich food history to discover. Before starting this book, I hadn't
the foggiest notion of who Philippe Mathieu was, even though I had
eaten his signature creation dozens of times. Mr. Mathieu is credited
with two things: starting the first brick-and-mortar restaurant in Los
Angeles way back in 1908 and, seemingly by accident, creating the
French dip sandwich. In that same year, Henry Cole opened his own
saloon, complete with a 40-foot mahogany bar and tables pieced together
from old trolley cars. He, too, claimed to have created the French dip.
Not only did the two restaurants open in the same year, blocks apart
from each other, but they also served the same delicious sandwich. A
rivalry was born that is still alive and well today. Heck, now you can get
a French dip in easily a hundred restaurants in this city. But those are still
the only two that matter.

By the 1920s, LA was already dotted with classic taverns: the Musso &
Frank Grill, Pacific Dining Car, Tam O'Shanter, and the Pantry. Every

night of the week, you could hop into your vintage car (cars here never rust, which is cool because rust never sleeps, which means your car never sleeps, logically) and visit a different hotspot.

As fantastic—and still thriving—as those Old Hollywood places were and are, they're growing a little long in the tooth. The menus, decor, and even some of the waitstaff look pretty much the same as when they first opened. The fact is, the culinary scene in LA stagnated for years until fairly recently. Sure, Wolfgang Puck blew some celebrity minds when he decided to toss BBQ chicken on top of a pizza in the eighties. But a food scene cannot survive on alfalfa sprouts and mashed yeast alone.

Today, Los Angeles is a cultural hodgepodge, with disparate, clearly defined neighborhoods such as Chinatown, Little Ethiopia, and Thai Town. A person could (and can and does) eat a different regional cuisine on adjacent streets on the same day. And while soaring NYC rental prices are bad for Big Appletons, they've been a blessing for LA, as chefs and restaurateurs have ditched the East Coast for palm trees and sunshine. Nowadays, chefs are almost as famous as the movie stars they feed.

Inside this book you will not only learn about where to eat for

Pearl's BBQ

Sqirl

breakfast, lunch, and dinner, but how each restaurant (or truck) is an extension of the man or woman who created the dish. From local hero chef and social activist Roy Choi to Nancy Silverton to Wes Avila, the latter of whom perfected the taco while operating out of a pop-up stand. Now, Avila has his own storefront and it's lit! Another line to beat.

Use this book as a kind of cheat sheet to the best food this great city has to offer. And if you happen to see me sitting nearby—most likely eating a piece of pie—feel free to come over and say hi. But that's all. I take pie-eating pretty seriously.

—Mike Postalakis

PRICE CODE KEY FOR MAINS

$ = less than $10

$$ = $11–$30

$$$ = $31–$50

$$$$ = $51 and above—Obviously you've got the funds to cover this.

1

BREAKFAST CAN'T WAIT!

"A bachelor's life is a fine breakfast, a flat lunch, and a miserable dinner."

— *Francis Bacon*

Ever since I moved into a tiny apartment (on the bright side, it's really expensive) in the once *Swingers*-iffic neighborhood of Los Feliz, I've noticed that the repast I most enjoy is the first one. Though you may have also heard that this is the most important meal of the day, that dubious claim was in fact made in an article written close to a hundred years ago in a magazine edited by one Dr. John Harvey Kellogg, who *coincidentally* had a profitable side business in the flaked cereal market. There's a cornflakes-loving sucker born every minute, apparently.

Whatever its importance, breakfast has a number of upsides. For starters, you can have it whenever you like—even for starters. Many menus will tell you "Breakfast served all day." Which means nobody will give you (sunny) side-eye if you order an omelet at 11 p.m. Rise and shine!

THE BEST ALL-AROUND BREAKFAST SPOTS

SQIRL

$$

720 N Virgil Avenue

SILVER LAKE

323-284-8147

sqirlla.com

Feeding the hippest of Silver Lake's hipsters since making the transition from jam preserve brand to full-fledged cafe circa 2012, Jessica Koslow's eatery has left an indelible stamp on the rejuvenated brunch scene in LA.

Equally at home dishing out vegan treats or frying up bacon, Sqirl offers something for every Bad Hombre and Nasty Woman. They even serve breakfast salads! That's a salad constructed with breakfast items. What a time to be alive!

But if you want my advice—why else did you buy this book?— go with the Green Eggs and Jam: country bread, creamed spinach, onion jam (their specialty), fried egg, and arugula. I guarantee your grandmother never made anything close to this good. Or at least mine didn't. My grandmother was an ace at opening cans of Campbell's Soup.

There's also the splendid Sorrel Pesto Rice Bowl featuring a poached egg, watermelon radish, feta cheese, and a preserved lemon all sitting on top of Kokuho brown rice and a dash of sorrel pesto sauce. You're gonna want to splurge and add some bacon to that bowl. Obviously.

Every harvest moon or so Sqirl features a BBQ Carrot Socca Pancake,

Sqirl

which sounds like a game of culinary Mad Libs (even I, a soon-to-be bestselling food writer, had to look up what Socca was—it's chickpea flour). Also recommended is the millennial's scourge, Avocado Toast. The toast comes adorned with hot pickled carrots and green garlic crème fraîche, which I believe is French for "fresh cream."

The coffee game here is top-notch as well. Try a cappuccino with their house-made almond milk. Take your capp and breakfast salad around the corner, to their patio, and eavesdrop on all the young people talking about how much they YOLO'd the weekend away.

Several lunch items are choice as well. I know, I know—this is the breakfast section. I'm already breaking the rules. But I just can't help it. I'm a sucker for sandwiches, and I simply heart-emoji the Jamon Pepín: house ham, beurre de baratte, country mustard, and comté.

A writer at a renowned food magazine called the Kabbouleh, a crisped rice and kale combo, "the vegetal equivalent of a viral video." And while I couldn't agree more that the Kabbouleh is super yummy, this is the sort

Sqirl

of incomprehensible description that a) tells you nothing about the food itself and b) makes me feel stupid. It's the reason, in other words, I wrote this book.

GJUSTA

$$

320 Sunset Avenue

VENICE

310-314-0320

gjusta.com

Gjusta is the new king of Westside breakfast, with more-than-ample seating and Instagram-worthy pastries (that somehow manage to taste as

good as they look). Since they serve breakfast till 5 p.m., you can't really go wrong with anything on the menu. Standout dishes include Polenta Baked Egg with asparagus, spinach, and ricotta. If your trainer is looking over your shoulder, then go with the Grain Bowl, which is brimful of goodness: kimchi, greens, fermented turnip, soft egg, and a choice of salmon or avocado. A perfect post-hot yoga meal.

Also perfect: the Lox & Fried Egg with crispy potatoes. It's my go-to, and if you're as bad at hot yoga as I am, it'll be yours too.

TOP TEN CAPPUCCINOS

The Euro-trash-lite lifestyle suits me just fine: hanging out in cafes, an important book open on your table (I've half-read some of the greatest novels of all time), a bottomless cup of coffee at your side.

So, yeah, here's where you go for a great cappuccino. Tell them Slavoj Žižek sent you.

10. Caffe Vita (Silver Lake)

9. Alfred in the Alley (West Hollywood)

8. République (Hancock Park)

7. Sqirl (Silver Lake)

6. Figaro (Los Feliz)

5. Maru Coffee (DTLA)

4. Dinosaur Coffee (Silver Lake)

3. Stories Books & Cafe (Echo Park)

2. G & B (DTLA)

1. Intelligentsia (Venice)

Figaro

THE BEST BREAKFAST BURRITOS

MAGNOLIA GRILLE

$$

10530 Magnolia Boulevard

NORTH HOLLYWOOD

818-766-8698

themagnoliagrille.com

This old-school neighborhood diner dishes out one hell of a corned beef hash breakfast burrito—equipped with sides of avocado and sour cream. With its red vinyl booths, weathered carpet, and KLOS blaring on the speakers, I half-expected to see Mickey Rourke and Steve Guttenberg hanging out. You need this wrapped breakfast treat in your life.

COFAX

$$

440 N Fairfax Avenue

FAIRFAX

323-424-7485

cofaxcoffee.com

I really only love two things in this world: KISS and hash browns. OK, three things—since Cofax puts hash browns in their burritos. Why don't more places put hash browns in their breakfast burritos? The world would be a much better place.

Cofax has a few different burritos to choose from—variety is the spice of life, after all. Speaking of spice, their chorizo burrito has a definite kick to it. You can also go with the classic bacon-filled burrito. There's a vegetarian option as well, in case you swing that way. On lucky days, they might be serving the pastrami burrito. Always worth calling ahead for availability of that one. And recently they've included a hot link burrito which features cased meats sent straight from BBQ giant Bludso's in Compton. So many great burritos to choose from, what's a food writer to do? Order all of them, duh.

Oh yeah, and these breakfast behemoths are served ALL DAY. So the early bird may get the worm, but us snoozers can settle for a darn good breakfast burrito.

STAMP PROPER FOODS

$$$

4500 Los Feliz Boulevard

LOS FELIZ

323-953-5181

stampproperfoods.com

Trying to make food that is inherently unhealthy into a healthy dish usually means a real sacrifice in taste. But Stamp Proper Foods in Los Feliz, which prides itself on only using organic ingredients, manages to save the flavor. This flavor-saver is filled to the brim with fluffy, soft scrambled eggs, turkey bacon, black bean mash, cotija cheese, and crispy golden potatoes. A bit on the pricey side, and, tbh, you usually lose me at turkey bacon, but I guess you make up for that price in fewer medical costs down the line.

JINKY'S CAFE

$$

14120 Ventura Boulevard

SHERMAN OAKS

818-981-2250

jinkys.com

Rarely do I find myself in Sherman Oaks but when I do, I always stop by Jinky's Cafe. Their motto is "better than breakfast in bed." Not sure I agree with that, but I'm easygoing and am willing to give Mr. or Ms. Jinky the benefit of the doubt. You'll want to order the Desperado—named after the Eagles' song, for reasons that I found less than obvious.

This burrito comes correct with scrambled eggs, red onions, tomatoes, and Ortega chilies. An excellent pairing: their turkey-chicken chorizo with a scoop of pea guacamole, salsa, and sour cream. You won't have "Heartache Tonight." This is another not entirely apposite Eagles reference, but once you start, it's surprising difficult to stop. I guess that's "Life in the Fast Lane."

TACOS VILLA CORONA

$

3185 Glendale Boulevard

ATWATER VILLAGE

323-661-3458

The Blessing of Bourdain transformed this tiny hole-in-the-wall Mexican family joint, long famous in the Atwater Village community for one of the best breakfast burritos in town. After being featured on the renowned chef's show, their cover was blown. Long lines formed. A quick grab-and-go bite before work became something you had to

Tacos Villa Corona

schedule before or after (or, in my case, instead of) pilates. On the bright side, there's a pet store next door that specializes in exotic birds, so while you wait for your bacon and papas burrito, you can go inside and pet a parrot. Parrots love that kind of thing.

LUCKY BOY DRIVE-IN

$$

640 S Arroyo Parkway

PASADENA

626-793-0120

luckyboyburgers.com

The sheer size of Lucky Boy's burrito puts it on a list of its own. You'll feel like the star of one of those food challenge shows—you know, the ones where the host tries to stuff a nine-pound burger down his gullet. It's like that, except you don't get paid to do it. My advice: Share with a friend. Or don't—go ahead, take on the challenge. They're your arteries. Go for the gold with the double meat (bacon and sausage) burrito.

NICK'S CAFE

$$

1300 N Spring Street

CHINATOWN

323-222-1450

nickscafela.com

Back in the old timey days, Chinatown used to be called China City— until the late 1940s, after numerous fires devastated the neighborhood. The area was then rebranded as Chinatown. That's when a most-certainly-not Chinese man named Nick opened his own diner. It has since become a cop hangout (is there a safe space where robbers can grab a bite?) that also happens to make a killer breakfast burrito. There's usually a rush on the weekends, so go during the week—they open at

5:30 a.m. It'll most likely be you and a bunch of LA's finest talking about the thin blue line between crime and the American Dream. What's not to love?

Nick's Cafe

TACOS TU MADRE

$$

1824 N Vermont Avenue

LOS FELIZ

323-522-3651

tacostumadre.com

This place scores bonus points by being literally across the street from my apartment. And they don't *seem* to mind me wearing my bathrobe in line. But I wouldn't list their breakfast burrito here if it wasn't also freakin' delicious. They serve a pastrami burrito at salami prices—it's also packed with bacon, fried egg, mozzarella cheese, and green-as-green-can-be guacamole. Heaven in a tortilla is what I would call it if I were given to corny expostulations.

Tacos Tu Madre

PATRA'S

$

2319 San Fernando Road

ECHO PARK

323-225-9944

patrasburgers.com

Echo Park has a long and storied history, serving as the launching point for hundreds of formerly starving artists (musicians, actors, writers) as well as the sort of less savory aspects that usually accompany what passes for dirt-cheap rent in Los Angeles. It also, unsurprisingly, features some hidden gems among its restaurants. This local institution serves tasty hamburgers, pollo and asada plates, and one of the best breakfast burritos anywhere. It's also one of the least expensive meals on this list—less than five dollars! Seriously, they're practically giving these things away. The #26 with chorizo is the way to go.

RICK'S DRIVE IN & OUT

$

2400 Fletcher Drive

SILVER LAKE

323-660-5988

Sure, the name of the place sounds like an old porno you might find in a dusty box of VHS tapes in the corner of your dad's garage, but unlike that relic from a more or less innocent past, this place delivers the goods.

Located on the invisible line that splits Silver Lake and Frogtown, Rick's has been the go-to place for chili fries, onion rings, and other (literally) heart-stopping goodies since time immemorial, or when I moved here, which amounts to the same thing. The breakfast burrito represents a master class in the no-frills approach to burrito construction—just bacon, ham, or sausage wrapped in a warm tortilla filled with rice and beans. That's it. And that's all it needs to be considered the best.

Rick's Drive In & Out

THE BEST DINERS

BRITE SPOT

$$

1918 Sunset Boulevard

ECHO PARK

213-484-9800

britespotdiner.com

No place in LA has been on and off my "best-of" list more than Echo Park's lone red booth diner. Despite constantly changing hours (used to be 24/7; now it's only open till 3 p.m.) and inconsistent meal quality, I keep coming back to Brite Spot. The thing is, when it's good, it's *really* good. Their Southern Decadence is a calorie-packed behemoth: chicken-fried chicken, bacon, and a buttermilk biscuit, smothered in Cheddar and sausage gravy, with a sunny-side egg on top. But the real showstopper is the in-house pie, baked daily. You can't go wrong with any of the selection on offer, but the thick and crunchy pecan or the salted honey hold pride of place in my book. Now here's hoping they change back to a late-night spot. Who has a hankering to eat pie in the middle of the afternoon? Besides me and Quentin Tarantino—or QT, as I like to call him, but never to his face, because he doesn't know me and that would be rude.

THE ORIGINAL PANTRY CAFE

$

877 S Figueroa Street

DTLA

213-972-9279

pantrycafe.com

The Pantry never closes. Not even on holidays. In fact, they don't even bother ever locking the doors. Anybody with an appetite can waltz right on in there and grab a booth. Or sit at the counter like a real regular. Like me.

The Pantry is a fine place to eat a giant stack of pancakes on the cheap, drink a cup of black-as-dark-matter coffee, and peruse all the different varietals of human and semi-human inebriation that manage to stumble through the doors in the wee hours. You've got your weekend warriors, down from the Valley to catch a Kings or Clippers game (Lakers tix, even when the team struggles, are impossible to get), bachelor/bachelorette party revelers, or just the usual down-on-their-luck Skid Row drunks. All are welcome here (to a point—there's an on-site security guard should anyone get too rambunctious).

OK, so it's late, you're lit or turnt up or whatever the phrase is: what should you order? Well, that depends on which poison you picked that night. Did you do a bunch of tequila shots while yelling "Woo-hoo"? Probably best to go with the aforementioned pancakes. Helps soak up the belly full of liquor. Did you shuffle your way, hands in pockets and a hat full of rain, from the legendary King Eddy Saloon? Bacon and eggs will cheer you up. Or do you fancy yourself the next Don Draper, cool demeanor matched with a slick suit? You're in luck—they have a T-bone steak the size of your perfectly-in-check ego.

After you've finished your meal, go pay at the cashier's booth, where you'll notice the worn-down linoleum from the footsteps of a million night owls before you. Cash only.

HOUSE OF PIES

$$

1869 N Vermont Avenue

LOS FELIZ

323-666-9961

houseofpiesla.com

The name should clue you in to everything you need to know about this Los Feliz greasy spoon. HofP is best experienced at the witching

House of Pies

hour, after the bars have closed and the open mic-ers have bombed. You're likely to find customers burying their faces in a mountain of (really good) onion rings or one of the two dozen pies they bake on the reg. Like all yet-to-be demolished relics of old LA, there are a bunch of myths surrounding this place. Rumor has it Quentin Tarantino wrote (and I mean wrote—with a pen and everything!) *Reservoir Dogs* in one of these booths, a plate of key lime pie his only loyal friend. Maybe it's true. Doesn't really matter.

My go-to is a slice of pecan pie. The waitstaff are always super friendly, and more than willing to refill cup after cup of coffee as you hang out musing on the vicissitudes of life in the City of Angels. Or writing *Reservoir Dogs 2* with a pocket full of ballpoints. Important note: House of Pies used to be open all night, but now closes at the still-reasonable hour of 3 a.m. on weekends, 2 a.m. on weekdays.

NICKEL DINER

$$

524 S Main Street

DTLA

213-623-8301

nickeldiner.com

My father once said, apropos of nothing, that "all the great breakfast joints are downtown." Weirdly, though he has lived his whole life in the Midwest, he was right. At least in Downtown LA. The best, if not *the* best, breakfast spot is on Main Street. A stone's throw from Skid Row. That's where you can find the Nickel.

The ghost of a former fried chicken shack still permeates the walls here, which is maybe one reason they serve a fried chicken dinner—best to keep the spirits happy. Before the chicken shack, the spot was a small cafe called The Circus. A mural of the old menu is still displayed, including the prices. Nineteen cents for a hot dog! If I had a time

Nickel Diner

Nickel Diner

machine, I'd go back and buy 10 of those encased delicacies. Right after I killed Hitler, of course.

My favorite meal at the Nickel is a BBQ hash called 5th and Main. It's a couple of soft poached eggs on top of tender pulled pork and chunky potatoes. It's as hearty as something without an actual heart can be. (It's possible I don't quite understand the etymology of "hearty," but this is not a book about etymology. I'm pretty sure.)

Got a big appetite after a night of train hopping? Then go with the 10 Cents Bag. That's a flat iron steak that comes straight out of a William Kennedy novel, with a side of eggs and potatoes. FYI: It doesn't cost 10 cents. That would be, like, one penny per ounce of meat.

The treats at the Nickel are also special. Their Maple Glazed Bacon Donut is a huge seller, and for good reason. Additionally, they'll bring to your table a selection of various high-calorie confections. I've tried them all. I've also tried on different size pants over the years. No regrets.

The Nickel feels like old LA. The booths are lived in, and the ceilings are high in that grand architectural tradition. The neighborhood, truth be told, can feel a little sketchy. But like most every neighborhood in Los Angeles these days, that's changing quickly. It's like Heraclitus said (paraphrasing): Change happens. But as long as the BBQ hash, the donuts, and flat iron steaks stick around, we'll all be fine.

THE 101 COFFEE SHOP

$$

6145 Franklin Avenue

HOLLYWOOD

323-467-1175

101coffeeshop.com

Formerly known as the Hollywood Hills Cafe (made famous in the final scenes of the movie *Swingers*), this coffee shop was taken over more than a decade ago by Warner Ebbink and Brandon Boudet. They kept the hipster decor: golden leather booths, jagged rock walls, and heavy stainless-steel silverware. It's full-on sunny-California-in-the-'60s: look to your right, kids—it's Brian Wilson!

The 101 (so named because the freeway is right next door) knows what it is: a gosh-darn diner that serves gosh-darn diner food. Browse the menu and you'll see all the familiars: pancakes, two eggs any way you want them, some sort of oatmeal business. The basics.

The Mikey Fitz always does me right. A perfect setup of eggs (over medium), two pieces of either bacon or sausage, and three pancakes (or French toast). On the opposite of the plus side, the 101 serves diner coffee. Which means . . . well, there are plenty of good coffee shops in the area.

The reason I recommend the 101 is not really breakfast-related, to be honest. The 101 is featured here for its milkshakes. Holy moly are they delicious! Get the Purple Haze shake. Named after the most famous song by the second-greatest guitarist of all time (where's the Ace

machine, I'd go back and buy 10 of those encased delicacies. Right after I killed Hitler, of course.

My favorite meal at the Nickel is a BBQ hash called 5th and Main. It's a couple of soft poached eggs on top of tender pulled pork and chunky potatoes. It's as hearty as something without an actual heart can be. (It's possible I don't quite understand the etymology of "hearty," but this is not a book about etymology. I'm pretty sure.)

Got a big appetite after a night of train hopping? Then go with the 10 Cents Bag. That's a flat iron steak that comes straight out of a William Kennedy novel, with a side of eggs and potatoes. FYI: It doesn't cost 10 cents. That would be, like, one penny per ounce of meat.

The treats at the Nickel are also special. Their Maple Glazed Bacon Donut is a huge seller, and for good reason. Additionally, they'll bring to your table a selection of various high-calorie confections. I've tried them all. I've also tried on different size pants over the years. No regrets.

The Nickel feels like old LA. The booths are lived in, and the ceilings are high in that grand architectural tradition. The neighborhood, truth be told, can feel a little sketchy. But like most every neighborhood in Los Angeles these days, that's changing quickly. It's like Heraclitus said (paraphrasing): Change happens. But as long as the BBQ hash, the donuts, and flat iron steaks stick around, we'll all be fine.

THE 101 COFFEE SHOP

$$

6145 Franklin Avenue

HOLLYWOOD

323-467-1175

101coffeeshop.com

Formerly known as the Hollywood Hills Cafe (made famous in the final scenes of the movie *Swingers*), this coffee shop was taken over more than a decade ago by Warner Ebbink and Brandon Boudet. They kept the hipster decor: golden leather booths, jagged rock walls, and heavy stainless-steel silverware. It's full-on sunny-California-in-the-'60s: look to your right, kids—it's Brian Wilson!

The 101 (so named because the freeway is right next door) knows what it is: a gosh-darn diner that serves gosh-darn diner food. Browse the menu and you'll see all the familiars: pancakes, two eggs any way you want them, some sort of oatmeal business. The basics.

The Mikey Fitz always does me right. A perfect setup of eggs (over medium), two pieces of either bacon or sausage, and three pancakes (or French toast). On the opposite of the plus side, the 101 serves diner coffee. Which means . . . well, there are plenty of good coffee shops in the area.

The reason I recommend the 101 is not really breakfast-related, to be honest. The 101 is featured here for its milkshakes. Holy moly are they delicious! Get the Purple Haze shake. Named after the most famous song by the second-greatest guitarist of all time (where's the Ace

Frehley shake?), the Purple Haze is made with vanilla ice cream, honey, blueberries, and bananas. It's sorta, kinda healthy. But it's every kind of delicious.

NAT'S EARLY BITE

$

14115 Burbank Boulevard

SHERMAN OAKS

818-781-3040

natsearlybite.com

They say "he who buys cheap buys twice." The breakfast at Nat's Early Bite, in the midsection of Sherman Oaks, is so cheap I'll happily buy twice. But just because the meals at Nat's are cheap doesn't mean they lack in any sort of yumminess. The cooks here can crack an egg with the best of them.

This is a sit-down-and-gab kind of diner, where old friends do the *New York Times* crossword together or bitch about politics—usually both at the same time. My favorite item from the menu is the Baja Omelet: chorizo, tomato, green onion, Cheddar, and beans with a plate of tortillas, if you feel like rolling it all up. Most days, I feel like rolling it all up. Some days, I don't. What can I say? I'm capricious.

PANN'S RESTAURANT

$

6710 La Tijera Boulevard

INGLEWOOD

323-776-3770

panns.com

Sitting in one of the white and red leather booths at Pann's, you might feel a sense of cinematic *déjà vu*. You offer your partner a piece of your bacon—they decline. "Pigs eat and sleep in their own . . . "

Ahhh, yes. In addition to being one of the better greasy spoons in the greater LA area, Pann's was also featured in *Pulp Fiction*. Movie lore aside, this place has some serious eats. Located near LAX, in the neighborhood of Inglewood, Pann's makes a great first or last stop on your visit to the City of Angels.

But this ain't no tourist trap. Plenty of locals squeeze their buns inside those vintage seats, chowing down on a Greek omelet or their signature Country Fried Beef Steak. Or you can mix breakfast and lunch (not to be confused with brunch) and try the Belgian Waffle and six wings. All the food here is pretty affordable and won't put too big a dent in your Bad Mother&%#$*@ wallet.

S + W COUNTRY DINER

$

9748 Washington Boulevard

CULVER CITY

310-204-5136

swdiner.com

A taste of the East Coast is nestled in the Sony Studios–adjacent neighborhood of Culver City. Let me start by saying this little dive has some of the best corned beef hash around. And you can get it two different ways: homemade or canned. Now, I know what you're thinking—"I should probably go with the homemade CB&H." Well, you *could* do that—it's still really good. But there's something indefinable I dig about that canned beef, so maybe give it a shot.

S + W also receives top honors for the way they cook their hash browns—always crisp, always to a golden hue. Nothing's worse than a plate of soggy potatoes. Another choice selection is the Two Eggs & Breaded Pork Chop.

The only downside: This place is tiny. Get there early or opt to sit at the counter. Otherwise, you could be in for a significant wait. Put your name on the list at the host stand and stroll over to Sony and pitch a new *Men in Black*. By the time your table is ready, it'll probably be in theaters.

THE BEST PANCAKES

I get it—you like to start the day with a nice, easy, healthy breakfast. Good for you. But for heaven's sake, you can't have sprouts and avocado mash every single morning. In the name of cheat day, I give you the best places for pancakes in LA.

BLU JAM CAFE

$$

15045 Ventura Boulevard

SHERMAN OAKS

818-906-1955

blujamcafe.com

How does this grab you—fresh blueberries, powdered sugar, Butternut Mountain Farm maple syrup? Sidebar: My Uncle Roy was from a town called Butternut. There's a funny limerick that accompanies that part of Ohio, but the twin dictates of good taste and the legal department keep me from quoting it here. Let's just say it involves some serious calisthenics. Anyway, the Blu Jam is seriously awesome. That's why it's on this list.

LITTLE DOM'S

$$

2128 Hillhurst Avenue

LOS FELIZ

323-661-0055

littledoms.com

Little Dom's does a very tasty Ricotta Cheese & Fresh Blueberry mash-up that will put almost anyone in a good mood. This Los

Feliz hipster-oriented eatery is (justifiably) better known for its non-breakfast menu items, but if it's pancakes you're after, you'll be more than happy.

DU-PAR'S

$$

6333 W 3rd Street

FAIRFAX

323-933-8446

dupars.net

Du-par's has been around for a long time serving pancakes to Angelinos, whether at the Studio City location (where Burt Reynolds made a passion-

Du-par's

ate speech about "filmmaking" in *Boogie Nights*) or the one at the Farmer's Market (which is the location listed above). In your mind's eye, and/or your mind's nose, when you think of pancakes—the crisp edges, the fluffiness of the center, and that *smell*—that's what you'll find at this diner. Flapjack aesthetics at their purest. And purely delicious.

JON & VINNY'S

$$

412 N Fairfax Avenue

FAIRFAX

323-334-3369

jonandvinnys.com

Chefs Jon Shook and Vinny Dotolo have enjoyed a meteoric rise to fame over the past few years, with their neighboring restaurant Animal being one of the most sought-after reservations in town. Their namesake joint has brought sexy back to Italian food with their meticulously crafted

Jon & Vinny's

pizzas and pasta dishes—but they also serve breakfast. And they do it well. The breakfast pizza is a hit with the millennial crowd (actually, ALL crowds love it), but for me, it's the buttermilk pancakes, which are accompanied with berries and a heroic scoop of butter, that deserve their own round of applause.

THE GRIDDLE CAFE

$$

7916 Sunset Boulevard

HOLLYWOOD

323-874-0377

thegriddlecafe.com

Located in the heart of the Sunset Strip, the Griddle is home to some of my favorite flapjacks. Believers in the occult might want to try the Black Magic: crushed Oreos inside the pancake, topped with whipped cream and even more Oreo cookie pieces. Also worthy of mention is the

The Griddle Cafe

Teacher's Pet: buttermilk pancakes with cinnamon apples baked inside. Need a little hair of the dog after a long night head-banging at the Rainbow Room? Then you should go with the Saturday Morning Fever, with its swirl of Baileys and Kahlúa.

My favorite pancake is the Eyes Wide Open, a shot of espresso and semi-sweet chocolate chips folded into the buttermilk recipe, with a sprinkle of powdered sugar on top. Leave your diet at the door—these are big portions.

OLYMPIC CAFE HOUSE OF BREAKFAST

$

3728 W Olympic Boulevard

ARLINGTON HEIGHTS

323-731-5405

With a name that long (and sort of confusing), these pancakes better be worth it. Rest assured, this Mid-City icon makes a meal out of "worth it." With possibly the crispiest pancakes on this list, you for sure won't be running any marathons after you eat. Or maybe you will. You've just loaded up on carbs, after all.

THE MUSSO & FRANK GRILL

$$$

6667 Hollywood Boulevard

HOLLYWOOD

323-467-7788

mussoandfrank.com

I was as surprised as you were to see this beacon of old-timey Tinseltown glamor land on the list. But, hey, you need something to soak up all the excesses of last night's starry revels. The pancakes here are big. Of course, they've been feeding the egos of stars and starlets since your parents were in cloth diapers. And you can't argue with the price—normally this place will set you back a few Jacksons (and I don't mean Tito), but you can get a nice thick stack of pancakes for $7!

FOOD

$$

10571 W Pico Boulevard

WEST HOLLYWOOD

310-441-7770

food-la.com

Simple is sometimes the best approach. For example: You want to create a classic breakfast staple for your menu. You decide on a no-frills ricotta-based batter, toss the batter on the griddle in perfect circles till they turn golden brown and fluffy, dice up some bananas and strawberries, and you have a damn near perfect—and simple—plate of 'cakes. Simple works. Except with restaurant names. Underachievers, please try harder. "Where do you suggest we go for the best pancakes on the West Side?" "Food." "Right, but where do you suggest we go . . . " Ad infinitum.

PIE 'N BURGER

$$

913 E California Boulevard

PASADENA

626-795-1123

pienburger.com

Might be time to add the 'n Pancake to the signage on this restaurant—the ones they serve up here are as good as the titular dessert and sandwich. These pancakes are of the thin and colossal variety. They look like golden-brown UFOs. This place also has one of my favorite counters to sit at and enjoy the theater of breakfast-making. If you have room in your stomach, try the boysenberry pie.

A-FRAME

$$

12565 W Washington Boulevard

CULVER CITY

310-398-7700

aframela.com

Every once in a while, you need to challenge yourself. Challenge your appetite. Challenge your love of pancakes. Culver City's A-Frame offers all these challenges. Good grief, they are not messing around here. On the weekends, for a mere $15, you can go with the all-you-can-eat (or till you burst, as they proudly proclaim on the menu) pancake special. And sure, you can have regular-style buttermilk pancakes, but we're pushing limits here, remember. Why not have a few pieces of Mochiko Fried Chicken to accompany your flapjacks? Also worth pursuing is the P.O.G.—which stands for Pineapple, Orange, and Guava. After a few helpings of both, your scale at home will be the one facing a challenge.

A-Frame

BRUNCH, BABY, BRUNCH

Need a hangover cure on a Saturday or Sunday morning? Here are my favorite brunch spots to get you through the weekend.

MAESTRO RESTAURANT

$$

110 E Union Street

PASADENA

626-787-1512

maestropasadena.com

Brunch is the newest add-on at this obscure Mexican eatery in Pasadena. After you've taken a selfie in front of the uber-cool neon sign reading "Dos Mas Mezcal!" I suggest ordering yourself the Chilaquiles—a non-movable feast of tortilla chips, eggs, red sauce, cotija, cream, avocado, and pico de gallo. It's so pretty, you might hesitate to eat it. Seriously, it looks like something Picasso might've painted—during his Brunch Period. There are minor masterpieces worth checking out too. I recommend the Chorizo & Egg Tacos or a breakfast Cemita. You can't go wrong with either. The bartenders also make one of the best margaritas in the city. Drink up, but you're responsible for any lost salt shakers.

BREAKFAST BY SALT'S CURE

$$

7494 Santa Monica Boulevard

WEST HOLLYWOOD

323-848-4879

breakfastbysaltscure.com

A spinoff of the popular burger and seafood joint located only a few blocks away, Breakfast by Salt's Cure wins the prize for best, most

Breakfast by Salt's Cure

perfectly cooked over-medium egg. Every time I visit, without fail, I get to tap open a yolk and watch as that gooey, yellow goodness slowly curls around my griddle cake—which is topped with whipped sea-salted butter and a dash of toasted cinnamon sugar. Also try the molasses-cured picnic ham. Oh, and the hash browns. Man, the hash browns are good. All griddle cakes can be made gluten-free if so desired.

CATCH LA

$$$

8715 Melrose Avenue

WEST HOLLYWOOD

323-347-6060

catchrestaurants.com

"Hey, there's what's-his-face! Why's he wearing that hat?"

"Oh, her new album is lit AF."

"I *hate* his movies. But, damn, he's fine."

These were the first things overheard the last time I sat down for brunch at this trendy-to-the-max West Hollywood rooftop spot.

Word of warning—this place gets *packed*. Prepare to wait. And for good reason. The food, to borrow a phrase from my mom, is lit AF. My advice: Book a reservation for right when they open, get there a tad early, and the hostess will lead you to an elevator that takes you to the roof—get ready for an amazing view of the city. Here's what you order: Smashed Organic Avocado Toast, prepared with pomegranate seeds, toasted almond slivers, a perfectly poached egg, all served on toasted seven-grain bread. They also do a mean Eggs Benedict.

WINSOME

$$

1115 Sunset Boulevard

ECHO PARK

213-415-1818

eatwinsome.com

Winsome is what it says it is. If you like Wes Anderson movies and anything with Zooey Deschanel except *New Girl*, this is your new go-

Winsome

to spot. First off, there's the Chia Pudding Bowl—a hearty portion of mango, pineapple, and coconut milk. If you've got a better way to start your morning, I'd like to hear it. Also popular is a Potato Rosti with Sunny Side Up Eggs. You can add on smoked salmon, house-made corned beef, or go with the veggie version (spinach and asparagus). But what really gets my taste buds budding is the Duck Egg Toast. Nduja, raclette, and oregano on rustic toast. You might not be able to say that three times fast, but you won't really need to, as the service at Winsome is excellent.

BADMAASH

$$

108 W 2nd Street

DTLA

213-221-7466

badmaashla.com

I need mention only one thing about Badmaash (aside from its awesome name). That one thing is Pork Belly Hash, topped with a sunny-side up egg with peppers, onions, tomatoes, and crispy potatoes, it goes swimmingly with an ice-cold chai latte. The father-and-sons culinary team here have done my belly right. I'm sure yours will agree.

BALTAIRE

$$$$

11647 San Vicente Boulevard

BRENTWOOD

424-273-1660

baltaire.com

For you fabulously rich types, Brentwood's Baltaire serves one of the best (and priciest) Benedicts in town. Two poached eggs on top of a tender prime filet—this is a steakhouse, after all—covered in hollandaise sauce and served with a side of duck fat potatoes.

Best of all, there's a sommelier on hand to help select a perfect wine pairing. Baltaire also has a fantastic open ceiling/patio area. Bring *all* the friends! Just don't get stuck with the bill.

THE BUTCHER, THE BAKER, THE CAPPUCCINO MAKER

$$

8653 W Sunset Boulevard

WEST HOLLYWOOD

310-360-6900

bbcmcafe.com

There's a lot going on at this West Hollywood hang—including that fun name. Try saying it real quick. See? Now hold your tongue while saying it. Just kidding. Use your tongue for tasting all the amazing brunch goodies. All of their Benedict options are served on fluffy buttermilk biscuits with a generous helping of sautéed potatoes. My favorite is the Avocado Benedict, which comes out exactly how you'd think: smooth, green, and tasty. The titular Butcher probably recommends the The Butcher's Eggs Benedict, and who would argue with a man holding a butcher's knife? Not this little piggy.

EAT

$$

11108 Magnolia Boulevard

NORTH HOLLYWOOD

818-760-4787

eatnoho.com

What's with these monosyllabic restaurant names? Pretty soon somebody's going to open a place called "MMM." Maybe I should buy that domain name now. Yeah, that'll bring in the big bucks!

Silly name notwithstanding, NoHo's Eat is a better-than-fine brunch spot featuring Frosted Flakes French Toast topped with fresh strawberries. Another option is the decadent Oreo Pancakes served with whipped cream. They also do a mean Corned Beef Hash. But I always go with something called Ned's Benedict. For the uninitiated, that's a plate of poached eggs, jack cheese, and avocado on a brioche bun instead of a muffin, smothered in hollandaise sauce. Excellent work, Ned! And like Ned, you'll be more than happy you ate at Eat.

BOTTLEFISH

$$$

11677 San Vicente Boulevard, Suite 200

BRENTWOOD

310-954-9495

bottlefish.com

I'm in Brentwood, fresh from the ATM, and in the mood for the new seafood-centric menu at Rick Rosenfield and Larry Flax's posh Bottlefish. If I still had a bae, I bet she would order the BAE Benedict with chile-glazed bacon, avocado, fried egg, and a house-made English muffin. But this place knows its ocean fare, so go with the Lobster Toast: toasted country bread with avocado mousse, lemon chili dressing, and radishes. The Smoked Trout Dip with their house-made "everything" crackers is a sure bet as well.

ASTRO DOUGHNUTS & FRIED CHICKEN

$$

516 W 6th Street

DTLA

213-622-7876

astrodoughnuts.com

Not since somebody said, "Hey, how about peanut butter AND jelly?!?" has there been a more revolutionary food combo than doughnuts and fried chicken. Amazing that humans have been around this long and we just got around to this breakfast nirvana. The doughnuts here at Astro are pretty incredible; the Maple Bacon is my personal favorite.

Astro builds one hell of a breakfast sandwich—in particular, the Fried Chicken Gravy. Here's how it goes: First, you pick a "bun," which is actually a savory doughnut. Then they pile on the fried chicken, smothered in sausage gravy. I always add a farm-fresh egg because it's 2019 and I plan on living forever. Pro tip: Wash this all down with a nitro cold brew coffee.

RÉPUBLIQUE

$$

624 S La Brea Avenue

HANCOCK PARK

310-362-6115

republiquela.com

Located in a building built and once owned by Charlie Chaplin, the French-centric République offers one of the most extensive—and

République

République

delicious—breakfast menus around. Their pork-belly-sausage–filled Breakfast Sandwich is as good a reason to get up early as you'll likely find. Another favorite is the Chorizo Sopes, which has scrambled eggs and chorizo with avocado, jalapeño, and black beans: A-plus. If you want something super healthy and quick, they offer a few fresh-pressed juices. The Purple Juice is made with carrots, beets, pomegranate, ginger, and mint. Or try a Green Shake with kale, green apple, cucumber, and avocado. The space, with its gothic arches, is big and beautiful, mostly sunlit, with some communal tables, perfect for all you morning people. There are a lot of you, apparently; this place gets packed early. But the service is quick, and the food is worth it.

TOP TEN PASTRIES

It's a go-go-go world out there. Sometimes, you just don't have the time to sit and eat your breakfast. For those of you in need of a quick morning nosh, I present the best pastries in the city.

10. ALL the Bagels at Bread Lounge (DTLA)

9. Maple Bacon Biscuit at Huckleberry Cafe (Santa Monica)

8. Apple Turnover at Milo and Olive (Santa Monica)

7. Meat Pies at Porto's Bakery & Cafe (Burbank)

6. Olive Oil Cake at Lincoln (Pasadena)

5. Matcha Croissant at WKNDR (Los Feliz)

4. Salted Caramel Pecan Roll at The Sycamore Kitchen (Fairfax)

3. Morning Bun at Proof Bakery (Atwater Village)

2. Ham and Swiss Croissant at Cafe Los Feliz (Los Feliz)

1. The Squash Muffin at Valerie Confections (Echo Park)

2

I NEED LUNCH!

*"Ask not what you can do for your country.
Ask what's for lunch."*

—Orson Welles

I've been described by many, many people as "out to lunch."
Which means there's nobody more qualified to recommend
the best mid-afternoon spots than yours truly. Whether it's
a quick grab-and-go sandwich or if you and your bestie
want to waste a whole afternoon gossiping about your
other bestie, LA has no shortage of daytime options. This
list combines some of the best between-bread, on-top-of-
bread, and sans-bread meals to be found in the city, most
of which are on the cheap—though a few might require you
to cash in half a bitcoin.

Like Noah's Ark, this list has almost every animal covered—from the cow (burgers), to the chicken (sandwich), to whatever you wanna throw on your pizza (pig's snout, anyone?). We will travel from Downtown to the Beach. Not in one day, mind you. We *are* talking middle of the day—that's easily 5 hours in traffic. So pick a neighborhood, pick a restaurant. I could steer you wrong, but I promise I won't.

THE BEST SANDWICHES

MEATZILLA!

$$

646 S Main Street

DTLA

213-623-3450

meatzilladtla.tumblr.com

Though rapidly gentrifying, elements of the old DTLA (what we now call Downtown Los Angeles) remain: there's still the smell of fried food from tempura stands and, on a summer day, the suffocating scent of pure, hot tar. After exiting the subway, a man tried to sell me a pair of brand-new argyle socks. Mismatched. Bummer. I thanked him anyway and headed down Main Street toward Meatzilla!, a back-to-basics burger joint—only hand-pressed beef patties, all ingredients fresh as can be.

From the orders of people in front of me, it's apparent that the BEEF! BEEF! Burger is the popular choice, but I go with The Yakuza! (Every sandwich has an exclamation point after it, but you don't have to shout. I do, but you don't have to.) The Yakuza! is a powerhouse of Katsu fried chicken, applewood bacon, tomato, fried egg, minced onion, green cabbage slaw, and tonkatsu spread. I'm assuming it was also named after the great Paul Schrader flick about the Japanese mob. Perhaps I'm wrong. First time for everything.

Meatzilla!

AUTHOR'S PICK · AUTHOR'S PICK

LANGER'S

$$

704 S Alvarado Street

WESTLAKE

213-483-8050

langersdeli.com

In the August 19th, 2002, issue of *The New Yorker,* Nora Ephron (herself a native New Yorker) caused a stir when she declared the hot pastrami

Langer's

sandwich at Langer's deli in LA " . . . the finest hot pastrami sandwich in the world."

To some it was considered treason, an offense ranking just below an East Coaster preferring Chicago deep-dish pizza over a foldable slice from Famous Ray's in the East Village. The article kicked off a famous debate over which Jewish deli in these United States of America serves the best cured meat. Some went to bat for Katz's Deli, located in Manhattan's Lower East Side, also known as the place where Meg Ryan faked an orgasm to Billy Crystal's mixed horror/delight in *When Harry Met Sally*. Some local Angelenos even voiced support for Langer's Fairfax District rival, Canter's, a place Guns N' Roses were known to frequent back before *Appetite for Destruction* ruled the airwaves.

While you can make an argument for the alternatives, there's really no debate. Ms. Ephron was absolutely correct: the hot pastrami sandwich at Langer's is the best of its kind.

Founded in 1947 by Al Langer, the deli sits just across from MacArthur Park, which is a great place to buy a fake ID while grooving to the Red Hot Chili Peppers, whose song "Under the Bridge," detailing singer Anthony Kiedis' former drug addiction, possibly references the area. MacArthur Park can be a less-than-savory neighborhood after dark, and the deli closes every day at 4 p.m., making Langer's the premiere lunchtime destination in the City of Angels. A turn-and-burn style delicatessen, you won't be waiting long for a booth. If you're flying solo, the counter is a great spot to read a newspaper while sipping coffee, just as Al Langer did day in and day out. There's even a small engraving at the first stool, his old spot. There's no ambient music piping through speakers at Langer's (or if there is, it's the Lawrence Welk type that I've learned to tune out). Just a cacophony of conversation from the customers, most of whom have been regulars for years on end.

Langer's has roughly 400 items on the menu—everything from pickled tongue to potato pancakes. So let me make it really simple for you: ask for the #19. From top to bottom, this sandwich is a handcrafted treasure.

Let's start with the unexpected: the bread. The bread for the #19 is just as famous as the meat that sits between it. What makes the bread famous is the fact that it is double baked. Every morning Langer's buys their rye bread from Fred's Bakery in Downtown Los Angeles, a tradition going on 40 years. The bread is first baked at Fred's, then it is re-baked at 350 degrees for half an hour at the deli. Then the bread loaves are kept in warming drawers, waiting to be sliced for sandwiches.

The next layer is Swiss cheese. Each slice is moist and tender. No hard edges. This addition, which you won't find on the Katz's or Canter's sandwich, offers a mild, sweet, and nutty component to the brininess of the pastrami.

Another unique element of the #19 is coleslaw. It's fairly no-frills: shredded cabbage, carrots, and mayonnaise. The slaw simultaneously adds crunch and softness. A perfect co-star to the main attraction—not unlike how Peter Lorre made every movie he was in better.

Speaking of the main attraction, let us now talk about the pastrami. The pastrami in the #19 comes to your table piping hot, bright pink, and a tad fattier than your typical New York deli would allow. When the pastrami arrives at Langer's, it is ready to serve and eat, cured and smoked at a meat wholesaler in Burbank, but Langer's steams their meat for an additional three hours, till it is tender enough to be hand-sliced. This allows for thicker slices. Langer's never uses a deli slicer to make their sandwiches.

The final touch on this masterpiece is the slathering of Russian dressing across the bread. Current owner Norm Langer, son of founder Al, says the dressing, which tastes very similar to Thousand Island dressing, acts like "a glue to hold the sandwich together." I'll admit the idea of glue in your sandwich doesn't sound very appetizing, but the sweet relish flavor really does tie the whole thing together.

Minus the booth of millennials with wax in their 'staches, the place probably looks the exact same as it did when Al first opened the doors. The #19 runs you $14.35, which is definitely not what it cost when Al first opened the doors, but in this economy, it's a fair price.

Now you're finished, full, and rethinking your critical evolution of Nora Ephron's body of work. You gotta hand it to the old girl. She was right. The sandwich is perfect.

PINK'S HOT DOGS

$

709 N La Brea Avenue

WEST HOLLYWOOD

323-931-4223

pinkshollywood.com

Rumor has it that on an otherwise ordinary Hollywood night in the 1970s, Orson Welles scarfed down a whopping eighteen hot dogs in one sitting at the legendary Pink's hot dog stand on Melrose Boulevard. According to noted director/Welles acolyte/ascot aficionado Peter

Bogdanovich, this simply isn't true. It was closer to seventeen. I kid, of course. But no one who's seen pictures of Welles' impressive '70s-era gut doubts that he had the ability to put away some weenies.

Pink's has acquired what the kids used to call a reputation around the City of Angels. Some people swear by it; others feel it's overrated—strictly a tourist destination. The tourist part is true. There's always a good number of out-of-towners in the formidable queue at Pink's, which is especially annoying at lunchtime when it's hot, because Pink's provides little refuge from the noonday sun—plus, people are awful. But if you time it carefully, or if you're lucky, the line will be short and you can grab a dog or two (or eighteen!) in a matter of minutes.

My go-to hot dog at Pink's is The Brando Dog, named for the actor who played Jor-El, Superman's dad, in *Superman: The Movie*. Apparently he was in other flicks as well. Unlike the man himself, The Brando Dog is a fairly uncomplicated meal: one stretch hot dog (nine inches) smothered in chili, Cheddar, and onions, with a dash of mustard. Not the prettiest thing I've seen on a plate, but the ingredients complement each other well. The Brando Dog is just one of many hot dogs named after celebrities that apparently frequent or have frequented or at least drove by the stand, an unprepossessing spot near the corner of Melrose and La Brea. Others include: the Rosie O'Donnell Long Island Dog (same as the Brando, but with sauerkraut); the Emeril Lagasse Bam Dog (stretch dog, mustard, onions, cheese, jalapeños, bacon, and coleslaw); and the Martha Stewart (stretch dog, relish, onions, bacon, chopped tomatoes, sauerkraut, and sour cream). Each has its merits, with the Emeril taking the Dog D'Or for best flavor combination. The Polish side of me just can't get behind sauerkraut—but then the Greek side of me hates olives, so go figure.

You can even get a hot dog named after the band Three Dog Night. The Pink's TDN is three hot dogs in one bun topped with cheese, bacon, chili, and onions. Enough to satisfy any rock star appetite.

Whenever somebody disses Pink's, I always retort with "the snap." And then, if I don't get arrested, I explain that all good hot dogs need "the snap." Pink's steams their frankfurters to perfection, causing the casing to stiffen, which results in an audible snap. No limp wieners here. (NB: It's impossible to discuss hot dogs without eventually venturing into soft-core porn slang.)

After you decide on a hot dog, the hardworking ladies (the stand is always womanned, never manned, for what I'm sure are reasons) will ask you to make another important decision: do you want fries with that? Or do you want onion rings with that? My sidecar is always the O-rings. The batter is slightly sweet, thick but still crisp. Pink's doesn't skimp on the amount of rings in a basket. You definitely get your money's worth.

And maybe, above all, that's Pink's greatest asset, and the grounds for its uninterrupted seven-decade run (it started as a hot dog cart in 1939):

Pink's Hot Dogs

its affordability. In a city where a cheeseburger the size of a thimble requires a second mortgage, Pink's has been feeding hungry locals and tourists since FDR created the WPA, which helped Orson Welles start his theater career, which in turn helped me write the first sentence of this piece. That's a New Deal everyone can get behind.

PHILIPPE THE ORIGINAL

$

1001 N Alameda Street

DTLA

213-628-3781

philippes.com

It's just past 7 a.m. I've been up for twenty-five hours. I'm close to delirium, yet I find myself the first customer of the day at Philippe the Original, near Downtown Los Angeles. I order a beef double-dip from a friendly counter lady. While she goes to retrieve my sandwich, I eyeball the freshly baked pies behind the glass counter. When she returns, I add a slice of pecan pie to my order. This is more or less what I order every time at Philippe's. I always enjoy it.

Philippe's history is intertwined with LA's own narrative. Considered the city's oldest active restaurant, Philippe's is also widely credited as the birthplace of the French dip. Local rival Coles, which opened its doors the same year as Philippe's, begs to differ, claiming it was the dip's originator. Each restaurant is fond of producing evidence to their claim (dated menus, newspaper clippings), but—full disclosure—I don't really care which sandwich came first: Philippe's French dip is superior.

The ambiance of Philippe's can best be summed up as Bukowski Chic. The cafeteria walls are covered with dusty framed photos of people long since dead, Dodgers and Lakers pennants, and neon signs for cheap beer. Toward the back, there's a row of private pay-phone booths in case you find yourself in a '40s-era noir film. Paraphrasing the late, great Lou Reed, it's a perfect place to "wait for your man." There's never been a time at Philippe's I haven't seen a Skid Row bum, or possibly a former member of the band Skid Row, asleep in one of the booths. This is strange, since Philippe's charges a paltry 45 cents for a cup of coffee. On the other hand, this does explain why it's a popular meeting place for AA groups. Did I mention Philippe's is great for kids, too? The kind in that Larry Clark movie—not actual children.

If this doesn't sound like your cup of (45-cent) coffee, then you probably don't read Charles Bukowski or listen to Lou Reed. That's fine. I've heard the French dip at Applebee's is better than expected. That's according to my mother, who, by the way, threw away my copy of *Transformer* when I was eleven.

Philippe the Original

BAY CITIES ITALIAN DELI

$

1517 Lincoln Boulevard

SANTA MONICA

310-395-8279

baycitiesitaliandeli.com

The west side of LA has its perks: the ocean, the beautiful Getty Museum, and the Godmother sandwich from Bay Cities in Santa Monica. As a would-be actor, I often find myself on this side of town for auditions, so after blowing yet another dog food commercial, I drag my low self-esteem into this deli and find solace in the Godmother, the quintessential Italian deli sandwich. Boar's Head ham, cheese, veggies, and slabs of mustard all packed between the homemade bread roll. Get it with extra peppers. The large "with the works" is still under $10. There are plenty of other great subs here, such as the Little Don Lorenzo with parma prosciutto, water mozzarella, pepper, basil, and tomatoes on a tiny baguette. I once saw somebody order the Tuna with the works. Different strokes for different folks, I guess.

Bay Cities also doubles as a grocery, so you can pick up a bottle of wine, some fancy cheese, and head down to the beach—live it up! As the great poet Prince Rogers Nelson once said, we could all die any day.

JOAN'S ON THIRD

$$

8350 W 3rd Street

BEVERLY GROVE

323-655-2285

joansonthird.com

Comfort. How do you define it? A favorite pair of sweatpants? An afternoon on the couch watching the PGA? Staring at the horizon from a rocking chair on the porch as the sun dips into oblivion? You sound lazy. This is how I define comfort: chunks of short rib meat, melted jack cheese, sweet red onions, and arugula on grilled country white bread.

That, folks, is heaven between bread. The Short Rib Melt at Joan's on Third was good enough to grace the cover of *Bon Appétit*, so I'm not exactly going out on a limb here when I say—at least in this one very particular instance—you can believe the hype.

HOWLIN' RAY'S

$$

727 N Broadway #128

CHINATOWN

213-935-8399

howlinrays.com

The buzz around the hot chicken sandwich at Howlin' Ray's is almost as hot as the actual sandwich. But the lava-red, deep-fried, covered-in-creamy-slaw-and-pickles thing itself more than meets expectations. And it had better, since the line to get in can be *long*. The line's just part of the experience, though, and the experience at Howlin' Ray's is almost on

Howlin' Ray's

par with the tasty food. The crew behind the counter is truly having fun doing what they love. Music is pumping; the crew is call-and-responding to orders in a military cadence, including stopping whatever they are doing to call attention to all the Instagrammers. The place is a freakin' blast. The spice level ranges from nonexistent all the way up to the eponymous Howlin'. Now, I love to sweat when I eat, but I had to dial back a little and go with the medium sauce. Even then, my Single and Lovin' It! T-shirt was soaked with perspiration. Sorry about that mental image.

LITTLE JEWEL OF NEW ORLEANS

$$

207 Ord Street

CHINATOWN

213-620-0461

littlejewel.la

A little slice of the Big Easy down in Chinatown. I was a tad skeptical when I first heard of this place. Everybody was telling me to try these amazing po'boy sandwiches. I lived in NOLA for almost 6 years. I ate my fair share of po'boys. But eventually, curiosity got the better of me and I

Little Jewel of New Orleans

stepped inside Little Jewel, ordered myself a Crescent City Fried Oyster Boy and—Lawdy Almighty! It was like being shirtless and on top of a horse (long story) on Decatur Street again! These perfectly fried oysters are nestled in a Nawlins-style French loaf, dressed with shredded cabbage, tomatoes, pickles, red onions, and mayo. The only thing that would've made this feel more like New Orleans would be a police ride to the drunk tank.

GUERRILLA TACOS

$$

2000 E 7th Street

ARTS DISTRICT

213-375-3300

guerrillatacos.com

For close to five years, Wes Avila had been operating Guerrilla Tacos as a pop-up taqueria, usually deep in the Arts District. Which was kinda illegal. He was always on the look-out for the fuzz. Now Avila has a brick and mortar place to call his own in the Arts District. Everything's legit now. The cops can't bother him anymore.

Success hasn't spoiled Avila. Most of the menu's greatest hits have remained, like the sweet potato tacos with fried corn and feta cheese. Another favorite are the wild boar tacos, topped with aged Cheddar. But Avila isn't resting on his laurels. In fact, one gets the sense that his pinnacle is still ahead of him. Lucky for us and lucky for our stomachs.

When I say Avila is serving up the best tacos in Los Angeles—a city that's not short on delicious Mexican cuisine—it's a little like saying that not only do I think LeBron is better than Michael (I do), but that when compared to LeBron, everyone else seems to be playing a different sport. Avila has changed the way I think about tacos. And I think about tacos a lot. Perhaps the more apt comparison is what people must've thought when they first laid eyes on a Picasso. Or saw KISS in concert. It's that revolutionary.

Here's the skinny on Avila: after giving up a promising career as a

Guerrilla Tacos

forklift driver, Avila paid his dues in a handful of kitchens around the city before he came up with the (then) novel idea of serving culinary-inspired street food. He borrowed a few Jacksons from family and friends, bought a cheap tent, found an inconspicuous spot downtown, and the rest is what this whole entry is about. Avila's tacos are complex yet unpretentious. There's a cabinet clearing vibe to his creations. He will literally make a taco out of any ingredient. Why not a fried oyster taco? Or a cauliflower taco with burnt tomato chilies and Medjool dates? This is how genius works, folks. Where most see a blank canvas, Pablo saw *The Weeping Woman*.

Painted on the front counter is the phrase "L.A. Don't Play." Designed by the Do Good Work firm, the interior of Guerrilla Tacos keeps those early street dwelling days alive—one wall is adorned with graffiti while another is exposed brick. In one corner is a stencil of the recently past (and early Avila champion) Jonathan Gold. A permeant seat.

At the bar you can order a salty margarita or a craft beer; wine is also available. The menu is constantly expanding, including pozole, tostadas, and albondigas soup. With his own spin on those classic dishes, of course. A recent Instagram post showed fresh Shigoku oysters. Good Lord. Just take ALL my money.

Guerrilla Tacos is story of a local boy making good. A story of not settling for the obvious, for taking chances, and, frankly, elevating simple street fare into something unforgettable.

JONES

$$

7205 Santa Monica Boulevard

323-850-1726

joneshollywood.com

Jones has been a West Hollywood hang for ages, serving up cocktails and cool vibes—not to mention one hell of a Meatball Hero. Mucho tender meatballs, fresh mozzarella, and Parmigiano on grilled country bread. Make sure you've got plenty of napkins on hand. And tucked into your collar. And you should probably lay a few across your lap. What I'm trying to say is Jones doesn't skimp on the marinara sauce. A delicious, slightly sweet sauce at that.

Enjoy this superhero of a hero sandwich in a corner booth under ironic velvet paintings. At least I hope they're ironic.

THE VILLAGE BAKERY AND CAFE

$$

3119 Los Feliz Boulevard

ATWATER VILLAGE

323-662-8600

thevillagebakeryandcafe.com

Few holidays reserve the right to have their own full-time, everyday meal. You never see a Flag Day Chicken Wrap, right? How about a Columbus Day Spaghetti & Meatballs? Nope, not happening. Thanksgiving, on the other hand, can be enjoyed guilt-free where and whenever you want. Especially at the Village Bakery in Atwater Village. This Turkey Day homage is served with all the fixings: turkey

The Village Bakery and Cafe

(obviously), stuffing, gravy, even fresh cranberry sauce. While eating this sandwich, I like to call my parents and sit through an awkward conversation about what I'm doing with my life. Then a bit of ugly back-and-forth shouting, till I'm a little sleepy from the meal, or my phone battery dies.

DIVISION 3

$

3329 Division Street

GLASSELL PARK

323-987-0500

divison3eats.com

I know we already covered breakfast, but I felt that the Corned Beef Biscuit Sandwich needed to be included here. It gets my vote for the best breakfast sandwich in town. And it's only $6. And you know what? Breakfast be damned! You can enjoy this sucker any old time of the day (or at least as the restaurant's hours dictate). I actually prefer it at midday. I'm cray that way. Whoa . . . that rhymed!

Anyway, located in the quickly gentrifying neighborhood of Mount Washington/Glassell Park, Division 3 is one of the best-kept secrets in LA. The similar-in-style sammie at Eggslut has gotten all the press recently, but trust your old friend here—this is the best between-bun (or biscuit) way to start your day.

BĀCO MERCAT

$$

408 S Main Street

DTLA

213-687-8808

bacomercat.com

There I was in the middle of a big Hollywood meeting, celebrities to the right of me, top-level executives to my left. And all eyes were on

Bäco Mercat

me! Even the beautiful starlet couldn't look away. And believe me, she wanted to. Was I holding court? Telling some witty anecdote about my time with the traveling circus? Nah, bruh. They were all gobsmacked at the Toron sandwich I had ordered. I flat-out *devoured* the oxtail hash, Cheddar tater, and tangy horseradish yogurt (most of which ended up smeared across my chin), all neatly wrapped in the house-made Bäco flatbread. I made an absolute fool of myself. Frankly, I've never been happier.

THE DARKROOM

$$

7302 Melrose Avenue

WEST HOLLYWOOD

323-931-3800

Hailing from the Midwest as I do, I'm always tickled by what Los Angeles considers to be a "dive" bar. Usually, it's a place with less-than-flattering light, a jukebox playing a Journey tune (unironically), and only a few craft beers on tap. My neighborhood bar back home had a tree growing in the middle of it. No joke. When the weather turned bad they couldn't open. We literally got rained out from drinking. There's no tree growing in the middle of the Darkroom, *the* dive bar in West Hollywood, but it is where people go when they wanna do some drinkin' and, maybe, when the lights go down, a little lovin', touchin', and squeezin'. Me? I go there for a little cheesin'. Grilled Cheesing, that is—yes, I'm aware that that was a lot of Journey puns to get through to get to an obvious joke. You know what's not a joke? The ultra gooey Cheddar, Fontina, and Muenster oozing out of the phonebook-thick garlic Texas Toast. I always welcome this monster with open arms. *Takes a bow*

PAPA CRISTO'S

$$

2771 W Pico Boulevard

PICO-UNION

323-737-2970

papacristos.com

All right! Finally something I'm an expert in—Greek food! What makes me such an expert, you snidely ask? Take a gander at my last name. I couldn't be more Greek if I were a slice of baklava on two legs. Which I sometimes think I am, but that's a story best reserved for my shrink. Papa Cristo's has been serving Greek cuisine at the same corner on Pico Boulevard for more than 60 years, importing wines and cheeses from the homeland. This place is known as "Athens in LA" (by me and a few of my friends, at least), and the lamb gyro has been the go-to wrap since the doors opened.

THE BEST PUPUSAS

Here are my favorite spots to grab this beloved Salvadoran dish.

5. Tita's Bakery (Hollywood)

4. La Numero Uno (Hollywood)

3. Jaragua (East Hollywood)

2. San Vicente Restaurant (Pico-Union)

1. Delmy's (Hollywood)

THE BEST BURGERS

In 2016, the Pasadena Chamber of Commerce unveiled a plaque in the sidewalk outside the LA Financial Credit Union dedicated to Lionel Sternberger. What did this scamp do to deserve a plaque? Well, supposedly, back in 1924, 16-year-old Lionel was the first person to ever slap a slice of cheese onto a hamburger patty. *Quod erat demonstrandum*, Lionel created the cheeseburger, then known as the 'Aristocratic Burger.' Bully for him.

As with any claim of a particular food's origin, we are left with the unreliable narrative of the past. There are two stories about Lionel's achievement: the first being that some well-to-do chap with 15 cents burning a hole in his pocket wanted a hamburger with 'all the fixings.' Lionel did as he was told, and piled on everything within reach, including a slab of cheese. The other story paints a slightly more dopey Lionel who, having burned one side of a patty, thus used the cheese to cover up his mistake. Either way, this doofus now has a spot with his name on it for your dog to use as a toilet.

Whether California (or Lionel) is the actual inventor of the cheeseburger, we certainly have perfected the art. So here are my go-to, must-have, flip-it-and-eat-it burgers in Los Angeles.

ANIMAL

$$$

435 N Fairfax Avenue

323-782-9225

animalrestaurant.com

So much for leading with subtlety—the Boner Burger at Animal will definitely swell your taste buds. Anything else is a matter between you and your spouse. Or doctor. This meat patty on marble rye toast oozes jack cheese and something called 420 sauce. Add on some caramelized red onion and poblano chili and it's about as sensual as a burger can get without, you know, the law getting involved. Head Animals Jon Shook and Vinny Dotolo know burgers. Spoiler alert: This won't be the only time they make this list. They also know you'll pay top dollar for their creations. The Boner Burger ain't cheap, but I'm here to tell you you're not gonna be able to order a more reasonably priced version from Canada.

BUTTON MASH

$$

1391 W Sunset Boulevard

ECHO PARK

213-250-9903

buttonmashla.com

I don't know about you, but playing video games always used to mean scarfing down Cheetos and pizza rolls while guzzling two liters of Mountain Dew. Well, my cardiologist said I can't do that anymore. Thank Kong for Button Mash! This arcade, located in Echo Park, likes to mix up Korean flavors with good old-fashioned guilt. Some other menu items include Coca-Cola-braised jackfruit and Spam-fried rice. Those items are all well and good, but this is the BURGER LIST.

And I'm here to talk about the Double Cheeseburger. No fusion going on here—this is a throwback to classic diner burgers. Ground chuck and sirloin blend, house-made pickles, Boston lettuce, and American cheese (!) all between a Bimbo Bun. At Button Mash, the phrase "burger time" has a double meaning—they have the '80s console of the same name. Game on!

Button Mash

FATHER'S OFFICE

$$

1018 Montana Avenue

310-736-2224

fathersoffice.com

If you're some sort of ketchup connoisseur, then you'll unfortunately find yourself SOL at this Santa Monica burger-and-beer haven. Oh, stop your bellyaching—we've come a long way in the condiment department. You can dip your fries in garlic aioli. It won't kill you. Father's Office's signature patty is The Office Burger, featuring caramelized onion, applewood bacon, gruyere, peppery arugula, and Maytag blue cheese. This burger almost makes me want to work in an actual office.

CASSELL'S HAMBURGERS

$

3600 W 6th Street

KOREATOWN

213-387-5502

cassellshamburgers.com

Cassell's still does things the old-fashioned way: using a meat grinder to produce their patties and cooking each to order under the original broiler. I enjoy my Cassell's burger with the addition of fried egg and chili con carne. Add on the lettuce and tomato fixings. This is where gourmet and good old simple grill work meet.

They offer a substitute vegan patty on any burger. Vegan options don't always work out well for anyone involved, but Cassell's takes pride in making a farro, mushroom, zucchini, miso, and flax patty. Topped with vegan cheese, it's pretty darn good.

IN-N-OUT

$

Various Locations

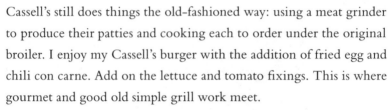

IN-N-OUT.COM

That is correct. I'm including a fast food joint's burger on this list. Did you seriously think I could include a list of LA burgers and not include In-N-Out? Hey, who doesn't love a cheap burger made fresh by a horde of (usually) young people dressed in all white? In-N-Out is as synonymous with LA as smog, traffic, and everybody in Starbucks writing screenplays.

Plus, they have a hidden menu to make your already-delicious burger extra yummy. Start by asking for the Double Double. That's two patties and two slices of cheese. Then say, "Animal-style, please." What happens next is a metamorphosis of Hulk-ian proportions. They'll not only mustard-grill your patties, but also add extra pickles and grilled onions, as well as another slab of Thousand Island spread. You can "animal style" your fries too (onions, spread, and cheese). Now go forth with this newly acquired knowledge and get animalistic with it! (You can also Google "In-N-Out Special Menu" to see the wealth of other options, but be warned: some of them are spurious and will only get you laughed at by the server who takes your order.)

HIGHLAND PARK BOWL

$$

5621 N Figueroa Street

HIGHLAND PARK

323-257-2695

highlandparkbowl.com

Gentrification strikes again, transforming LA's oldest bowling alley into a gorgeous, rustic palace of pins. It does cost a paycheck or two to secure a lane for an hour, and this isn't your mom and dad's bowling alley menu, with Calamari Fritti and Chicken Milanese.

Here you can find the Boomer Burger, featuring Fontina cheese,

Highland Park Bowl

heirloom tomato, Boston lettuce, chipotle aioli, and red onion. This is no gutter ball, which is almost but not quite a successful pun. Coupled with possibly the best fries around, this is the sort of burger Jeff Lebowski would consume between knocking down 7-10 splits. That is, if Jeff Lebowski actually had a job and could afford to eat here.

THE GOLDEN STATE

$$

426 N Fairfax Avenue

FAIRFAX

323-782-8331

thegoldenstatecafe.com

Always cooked to a precisely pink medium-rare, The Burger at this Fairfax District cafe is simple, no-frills, and always perfect. The boys at

The Golden State

Golden State pride themselves on using California-centric ingredients, which makes this burger a bit of a name dropper: Harris Ranch beef and Fiscalini Farms Cheddar. Add some arugula, garlic aioli, and ketchup, and you have a burger as beautiful as any sunset over the Pacific.

The friendly and knowledgeable staff will help you pair that patty with an ice-cold craft beer from their constantly rotating draft list. I pair mine with a nice tall Mexican pop. Not as hip, but just as refreshing.

PETIT TROIS

$$$

718 N Highland Avenue

HOLLYWOOD

323-468-8916

petittrois.com

Petit Trois' legendary burger, the Big Mec, is a gooey, messy, slapdash of a burger: two beef patties, cheese, and Thousand Island dressing, sitting on a buttery brioche bun. It literally melts in your mouth. And spills on your shirt. You *will* get sauce on yourself, so keep that in mind when dressing to come here.

BURGERLORDS

$

943 N Broadway

CHINATOWN

323-405-4012

burgerlords.com

Tucked away inside a Chinatown strip mall, Burgerlords' classic Double Cheeseburger brings all the patty lovers to the yard! This burger uses a custom tri-blend, grass-fed beef on a sponge bun, with lettuce, tomato,

Burgerlords

onion, and, of course, Thousand Island dressing. It's like a sassier version of the famous In-N-Out burger.

On the flip side of the spatula, vegans can find some yummy options, too. Made with a blend of grains and vegetables, this guilt-free patty could even satisfy the mightiest of carnivores, which I believe is a lion, but I'm no zookeeper. Yet.

EVERSON ROYCE BAR

$$

1936 E 7th Street

ARTS DISTRICT

213-335-6166

erbla.com

After leaving Osteria Mozza, chef Matt Molina opened this Arts District bar and soon gained a loyal following thanks to his Single Burger: prime

Everson Royce Bar

beef chuck, Tillamook Cheddar, and dill pickle on an egg brioche bun. The Single Burger is what Leo (da Vinci, not DiCaprio) must've been talking about when he said, "Simplicity is the ultimate sophistication." And that guy painted "The Last Supper," so he knows a thing or two about memorable meals.

If you can only try one cheeseburger in the City of Angels, this is the one.

THE BEST PIZZA

Los Angeles has long been behind other major cities when it comes to crafting a truly amazing pizza pie. New York is . . . well, New York. Long slices of cheese and/or pepperoni, folded and eaten while waiting for the subway. Chicagoans have their deep-dish pies, monuments of dough and sauce, usually with huge chunks of sausage buried deep in the pizza.

Inferior pie has been hanging over the heads of Angelenos like a cheesy, red-sauced Sword of Damocles. Sure, there was the mid-'90s success of chain restaurant California Pizza Kitchen, or CPK for short, but the shine of BBQ Chicken pizza soon faded.

Things are starting to turn around for the City of Angels, though. Chefs are beginning to take pizza seriously, and LA foodies couldn't be happier.

When Nancy Silverton opened Pizzeria Mozza in 2006, merging the craftsmanship of Naples with the experimental nature of New American Cuisine, the quality of pizza in LA started rising like expertly handled dough, and as of this writing, it is better than it ever has been.

Here is my list of the best places for wood-fired pies, deep dishes, slices on the go, and old school, *Sopranos*-style Italian joints. You'll fall in *amore* with each of them.

PIZZANISTA!

$

2019 E 7th Street

ARTS DISTRICT

213-627-1430

pizzanista.com

Don't let the late-night, Bowery drunkard decor fool you—yes, Pizzanista! is in thrall to an era of rock 'n' roll when singers covered themselves in peanut butter till they died and were eaten by rats. But

Pizzanista!

they take their pizza seriously here. This place was started in 2011 by a trio of friends, including world-renowned skateboarder Salman Agah, who recruited pizza savant Steve Samson, formerly of Sotto, to craft their artful pies. Using a 200-year-old sourdough culture from Naples, as well as California tomatoes for their marinara sauce, Pizzanista! offers a unique take on the New York pizza slice. Offer yourself up to the Meat Jesus: red sauce, mozzarella, Grana Padano, pepperoni, sausage, and bacon. It's the second coming of the carnivore-centric pizza.

PIZZERIA MOZZA

$$

641 N Highland Avenue

HANCOCK PARK

323-297-0101

pizzeriamozza.com

By now, what hasn't been said or written about Pizzeria Mozza? Praised by such luminaries as Jonathan Gold and the *New York Times*' Frank

Bruni, Nancy Silverton's Pizzeria Mozza was the game-changer LA pizza had been waiting for. Her pies—their crusts somehow both buttery soft and charred to a crisp; fresh ingredients laid on top (hand-delivered daily from the farmer who grew and harvested them); and finished off with a salvo of smoky flavor from her wood-fired oven—are unique in and of themselves, but are also part of a larger oeuvre. You can always recognize a Pizzeria Mozza pizza, the same way you can always spot a Picasso painting or a KISS song. There are many on the menu to choose from, and none will disappoint, from the Squash Blossoms, with tomato and burrata, to the Meatballs & Buffalo Mozzarella, with scatterings of fresh oregano. My favorite of her creations is the Goat Cheese, Leeks, Scallions, Garlic, and Bacon pie.

Pro tip: Their pastry chef, Dahlia Narvaez, is a James Beard Award winner. Save room for dessert, with such dishes as the Caramel Coppetta, with marshmallow sauce and salted Spanish peanuts.

BARONE'S

$$

13726 Oxnard Street

VALLEY GLEN

818-782-6004

baronesfamousitalian.com

I have an affinity for old-school Italian restaurants. I love red leather booths, white tablecloths, worn carpet, tacky lights hanging from the ceiling overhead, and, of course, pizza.

Barone's in the Valley has all of that in spades. This is the kind of place you would see in a movie, right before Joe Pesci whacks some snitch. I once sat next to *Boogie Nights* and *There Will Be Blood* director Paul Thomas Anderson as he and his lovely family dined on Barone's trademark rectangular pies. The cooks at Barone's don't skimp on the cheese, either. Every pizza is packed with an extra layer of gooey goodness. My topping of choice is their house-made sausage. Sweet with a bit of kick to it. *Delizioso!*

PIZZANA

$$

11712 San Vicente Boulevard

BRENTWOOD

310-481-7108

pizzana.com

The 48-hour fermented dough for these pies is smeared with red sauce from tomatoes straight off of Italian vines. After it goes into chef Daniele Uditi's curved oven, you get perfectly crafted Neapolitan-style pizzas. Since partnering with Candace and Charles Nelson, the couple behind Sprinkles Cupcakes, Pizzana is re-creating sleek yet casual dining in Brentwood.

There's plenty to choose from on the menu. One standout is the Carnivoro, topped with prosciutto cotto, spicy soppressata, fennel sausage, basil, and fior di latte—a semi-soft cheese imported straight from Italy. Having received lavish praise from *LA Times* food critic Jonathan Gold, be prepared to hear about Pizzana for years to come.

COSA BUONA

$$

2100 W Sunset Boulevard

ECHO PARK

213-908-5211

cosabuona.com

This is one of the newer additions to Echo Park, with a menu that features Smokey Mozzarella Sticks and Chicken Wings with gorgonzola dip. Chef Zach Pollack, owner of the exquisite Alimento in Silver Lake, is aiming here for an upscale version of the classic neighborhood Italian restaurant.

Like a scene out of *Moonstruck*, I fell hopelessly in love with their Biancoverde pizza, with ricotta, mozzarella, basil, spinach, and garlic. Each bite transports you to our sister satellite: this features a perfectly crisp yet still airy crust.

Perhaps you would describe yourself as somebody "completely enamored with animal protein." Then you'll probably want to go with the Meatlovers pie. This ode to flesh is loaded with pepperoni, sausage, and . . . wait for it . . . coppa, which is thinly sliced, dry-cured pork. But I'm sure you already knew that.

Lastly, Cosa Buona does a mighty fine Hawaiiana pie with pineapple, Canadian bacon, chiles, and smoked mozzarella. You'll have to provide your own leis.

JON & VINNY'S

$$

412 N Fairfax Avenue

FAIRFAX

323-334-3369

jonandvinnys.com

Like all great artists, Jon Shook and Vinny Dotolo's Italian eatery manages a delicate balancing act between the highbrow and the low-

Jon & Vinny's

down. Just like Jim Morrison. This is an apt comparison, if I do say so myself, since there's a pizza on the menu here named after one of the Lizard King's better-known songs. The LA Woman, with its one-pass smear of tomato sauce, thick globs of burrata, and fresh basil leaf, will certainly get your mojo rising.

The crust—nearly burned by the wood-fired flames—crackles with each bite, charred flakes floating in the air like memory's embers down to the snow-white paper table settings. Now *that's* poetry.

CASA BIANCA PIZZA PIE

$$

1650 Colorado Boulevard

EAGLE ROCK

323-256-9617

casabiancapizza.com

In business since the atomic age—with the decor to prove it—this Eagle Rock eatery features one of my favorite sausage pies around.

Sweetly anise-spiced and with cloves of garlic for balance, alongside eggplant and loads of mozzarella cheese, it's made with a thin, cracker-like crust.

Rumor has it that Casa Bianca was a favorite destination of future president Barack Obama during his enrollment at Occidental College. Our current president enjoys well-done steak with ketchup.

Anyway.

MASA OF ECHO PARK

$$

1800 W Sunset Boulevard

ECHO PARK

213-989-1558

masaofechopark.com

Masa is the Italian word for "dough," and in the case of this Echo Park family-style pizza joint, the dough is cornmeal. And delicious! It's the attention—and dedication—to the dough that makes these pizzas truly authentic Chicago deep dish. Each crust is 2 inches deep, more than enough to bear the weight of whole pear tomato and garlic-infused sauce, a layer of thick cheese, and, for my money, Masa's secret recipe sweet Italian sausage. This sucker takes roughly 40 minutes to bake and weighs approximately two phone books. You never "sausage" a thing! This deep dish will go down as a "pizza" of history. It's delicious every "thyme"! I can keep going. It's not like I "cannoli" talk in puns. But when I'm on a "roll," it's hard to stop me.

Editor's Note: You are in fact not on a roll. Stop.

VILLAGE PIZZERIA

$

131 N Larchmont Boulevard

LARCHMONT

323-465-5566

villagepizzeria.net

A transplant from our fancy-pants neighbor up north, San Francisco, this Larchmont area hangout has been producing true New York-style slices, as well as good old-fashioned '60s vibes, since 1997. This is actually my favorite place in the city to grab a slice and just hang out with a newspaper or a book. As far as slices go, I dig the Clam & Garlic. If you're looking for a whole pie, then I suggest the Village Special, which includes homemade meatballs, homemade sausage, pepperoni, onions, green peppers, mushrooms, olives, and anchovies.

You'll probably run into Steve, the owner. He's usually talking it up with customers; make sure you say hi. And if you have a whole day to burn, ask him how the Mets are doing.

MULBERRY STREET

$

15136 Ventura Boulevard

SHERMAN OAKS

818-784-8880

mulberrypizzeria.com

I've spent many nights curled up on my couch in the living room watching re-runs of *Friends* and enjoying (devouring) a large Fresh Spinach White pie, which is my go-to from this well-known Beverly Hills transplant, originally founded by Richie Palmer. I usually succeed, despite the certain knowledge that this particular pizza actually tastes *better* cold, the next day. This is still one of my favorite pizzas.

AND FINALLY ... BEST BBQ

PEARL'S BBQ

$$

2143 Violet Street

ARTS DISTRICT

pearlsbbqla.com

LA has a new king of BBQ. Owner Dana Blanchard's new Arts District spot is smoking up authentic central Texas BBQ, just like his grandmother used to do—the restaurant bears her name. The brisket is served juicy and tender, with a perfectly pink smoke ring. Oh, and it

Pearl's BBQ

smells amazing! Actually, the whole place, which is a big, open area with picnic tables, is a treat for the senses. You can even grab a seat next to the thousand-gallon smoker, personally made for Pearl's by the FatStack Smokers group.

On the menu, too, are beef short ribs by the pound and sausage links. Both are expertly done. Don't forget the side dishes: there's the customary potato salad, but I fell in love with their Southern-style coleslaw. This slaw has a kick to it!

The biggest surprise of all from my trip to Pearl's was their pecan pie. So soft and chewy, with big old chunks of pecans, and a crust so flaky I would never make plans with it. See what I did there? Apparently the recipe has been passed down over five generations! That's like 500 years of pecan pie perfection! Right? I'm terrible at math. You know what I'm *great* at? Eating pie. I'm a pro. And this is one of the best slices of pie in the city.

As of this writing, Pearl's is only open late morning till they're completely sold out of meats. And those lines can be looooong. It's like people knew I was gonna rave about this place before the book even came out!

Pearl's BBQ

3

MR. BAD EXAMPLE (HAPPY HOUR & NIGHT LIFE)

"Some like wine and some like hops. But what I really love is my scotch. It's the power, the power of positive drinking."

—Lou Reed

As an old, wise troubadour once sang, "It's always 5 o'clock somewhere." You've been working your knuckles to the bone, doing whatever menial task they throw on your desk, covering for that lazy bastard Henderson in accounting. 5 p.m.—a.k.a. happy hour—can't come soon enough.

etworking is sort of a big thing here, whether you're an actor, writer, producer, agent, agent's assistant, or maybe somebody not in the industry (even aspiring chefs and politicians have to mingle to get ahead). In a city this big, you soon realize one important fact: everybody is chasing the same ten jobs. Manage to nab one of those and you've got the golden ticket, brothers and sisters. The big brass ring, if you will.

But let's say you're not a person who wants to be surrounded by people persons, or maybe you're not all that interested in getting ahead in life. Maybe you just like to belly up to a bar, listen to the jukebox, and cry in your drink. No judgment here. Lord knows I've seen wilder days. Los Angeles has had its fair share of infamous drunks. From Fante to Bukowski, there's been a long lineage of angry poets willing to get themselves blotto in the name of their art. We'll visit some of their favorite watering holes. And maybe you too can sit on the same stool Hank Chinaski slid off of.

Alright, time to yell, "Yabba Dabba Doo!" and get yourself a stiff drink. Or a cold brew. Maybe one of those fruity, colorful drinks that need to be shaken a hundred times by bartenders with man buns. Whatever gets you through the night. Whatever you do, don't leave your credit card with an open tab. Classic rookie mistake.

And now, my guided tour (via Uber) of LA's best watering holes. Cheers!

CAFE BRASS MONKEY

$$

659 S Mariposa Avenue

KOREATOWN

213-381-7047

cafebrassmonkey.com

We're starting off with a karaoke bar. Gotta get the pipes warmed up— we've got a long night of shouting orders to barely-paying-attention barkeeps ahead of us. Plus, this place opens up early—like, right after breakfast early. So you can roll out of bed, throw back a Bud and a shot

of soju, and pretend you're Neil Diamond. I once saw a group of Japanese businessmen, all of them four sheets to the wind, sing the Ella Fitzgerald staple, "Let's Call the Whole Thing Off" together. Except when it came to the part "You like potato and I like potahto/you like tomato and I like tomahto/Potato, potahto, tomato, tomahto . . ." they never changed the pronunciation. It was so funny, I peed myself. Then everyone laughed at *me*, including me. Good times.

The KJ (that's Karaoke Jockey for the uninitiated) usually moves things along at a brisk pace, so put your song in, listen for your name, belt out your tune like Whitney at the Super Bowl, and afterward go back to drinking.

DRAWING ROOM

$

1800 Hillhurst Avenue

 LOS FELIZ

323-665-0135

Los Feliz's Drawing Room opens at the crack of 6 a.m. That's right. Your eyes ain't lying, which means you're not in an Eagles song. Let's get real, some of us (not me, of course) need a little hair of the dog the minute the sun makes an appearance. Drawing Room has been my personal drinking spot for nearly ten years. Even now, when I don't touch alcohol, I still like to sneak into the complete darkness of this authentic dive. Seriously, you can't see your hand in front of your face. The air is musty, the carpet worn completely down. There's a dragon mural on the main wall, which probably made sense whenever somebody decided to paint it. In other words, this place is beautiful.

The crowd here is good people; a lot of them crew on big Hollywood productions, working the overnight and wanting to ease into a morning's sleep with an ice-cold pop. Another saving grace of Drawing Room is that it's one of the last bastions of a real, disc-carrying jukebox. Not one of those god-awful digital satellite thingamajigs—the ones where a person can pull any song out of the atmosphere, whether somebody wants to hear it or not. Nope. Drawing Room keeps it old school—both in vibe and with the tunes. Tons of great old soul and funk, '70s rock, and a few (very minor) contemporary albums here. They also have two dartboards just in case you feel the need to get into an utterly pointless argument with somebody you don't know.

THE BEST MARTINIS

These places are money, baby! If you happen to see Vince Vaughn out in public, yell that to him, he *loves* it.

5. The Musso & Frank Grill (Hollywood)

4. The Dresden (Los Feliz)

3. The Three Clubs (West Hollywood)

2. Nick + Stef's Steakhouse (DTLA)

1. The Upper West (Santa Monica)

THE ESCONDITE

$$

410 Boyd Street

LITTLE TOKYO

213-626-1800

theescondite.com

Somebody once described this bar as "Skid Row adjacent." Umm . . . more like "in the dirty heart of Skid Row." But I'm not one to draw nice distinctions, and anyway it's fine—the parking lot is fenced in, not that there's really anything to be afraid of. This dive/music venue has a fantastic happy hour with cheap craft beers, cheaper canned beers, and even cheaper appetizers. Get down there for their Triple Treat Thursdays—a shot, a beer, and a BYO burger—which stands for Build Your Own. The food here is Chicago inspired, which is to say, delicious, high-caloric subs and fried foods.

They also have a homemade Mac n' Cheese with bacon and Ritz Cracker crumble—just like the way Mom made it!

FROLIC ROOM

$$

6245 Hollywood Boulevard

HOLLYWOOD

323-462-5890

Located smack dab in the heart of Hollywood, the Frolic Room just oozes nostalgia. For starters, it's hard to miss that old neon sign—like something out of a Cagney movie. In fact, I'm sure Cagney tied one on here back in the day. Many famous people frequented the Frolic Room. Charles Bukowski certainly did, as well as Elizabeth Short, a.k.a. the Black Dahlia, before she met her untimely (and infamous) demise.

The bartenders here don't cotton to these new-age mixology type drinks. This is a beer-and-shot bar. A place to mix it up with the locals. It's also right next door to the Pantages Theatre (our Broadway), in case you wanna slum it before going all highbrow.

My favorite part of the Frolic Room? They have a mural of old Hollywood types on the wall, done by the famous artist Al Hirschfeld. There are the Marx Brothers, Laurel and Hardy—and Einstein for some reason. Like life needs a reason.

FRANK 'N HANK

$

518 S Western Avenue

KOREATOWN

213-383-2087

What are some classic features of the "dive bar?" A fuzzy TV, usually tuned to a foreign soccer match or news channel; a jukebox with tunes better suited for porn soundtracks; a pool table with ripped felt and missing cue ball; and a dartboard with no darts. As Koreatown's premiere dive bar (can a dive bar be "premiere"?), Frank 'n Hanks checks the box on all those features. The bartenders are friendly, but not that friendly. They're not gonna make you a specialty cocktail. No way, José. This place does bottled beer and liquor and if you don't like it, tough. They carry a wide range of whiskeys, gins, vodkas, and rye. Enough to get you drunk.

TIKI-TI

$

4427 Sunset Boulevard

LOS FELIZ

323-669-9381

tiki-ti.com

I love the Tiki-Ti and all of their weirdly named tropical drinks: the Puka Puka, Uga Booga, and other assorted Hawaiian punchy concoctions.

It's a very small place, looks like an after-hours bar at Disneyland, and is often filled with long-time regulars, so get there early. Let's recap . . . Space to move around, no. Major credit cards accepted, no. Parking's impossible, too. And I'm still recommending it? Yes. I. Am.

THE TROUBADOUR

$$

9081 Santa Monica Boulevard

WEST HOLLYWOOD

310-276-1158

troubadour.com

Almost all of your album collection has played this stage. And while most of the iconic music venues have long been torn down, replaced with yet another Whole Foods or cell phone store, luckily, the Troubadour is still standing! This place has history, man. Lenny Bruce got arrested here for saying things that would be considered timid compared to what your 15-year-old niece posts on her Instagram.

Members of The Byrds met here at an open mic. Joni Mitchell, Gordon Lightfoot, and Neil Young all made their LA debuts at the Troubadour.

The booze selection is pretty standard. It's enough to get you drunk and out on the dance floor. So kick back and have a good time.

TOP TEN SINGLES BARS

Good luck out there, solider.

10. Edendale (Silver Lake)

9. The Otheroom (Venice)

8. The Bungalow (Santa Monica)

7. Birds & Bees (DTLA)

6. Alcove (Los Feliz)

5. Idle Hour (North Hollywood)

4. Seven Grand (DTLA)

3. Blind Barber (Culver City)

2. Ollie's Duck + Dive (Malibu)

1. Good Times at Davey Wayne's (Hollywood)

BIRDS

$$

5925 Franklin Avenue

HOLLYWOOD

323-465-0175

birdshollywood.com

Birds has a soft spot in my head . . . I mean, heart. This Franklin Village establishment has been getting people in the right mood since the go-go '90s. Located right next door to one of the premiere improv comedy theaters, Birds is a great place to grab a drink or two before seeing some of the best up-and-coming comedy stars (*ahem*, like yours truly). Most drinks during happy hour still cost under five smackeroos, and you should most definitely order the Happy Hour Nachos. Have them put EVERYTHING on it. You can survive on them for days. Trust me. You can also play Jenga. You know, the game that features the thundering sound of wood blocks crashing onto cement floors. Really does wonders for my anxiety. Bartender, can I get another round of nachos, please?

CHEZ JAY

$$

1657 Ocean Avenue

SANTA MONICA

310-395-1741

chezjays.com

Santa Monica's Chez Jay has been pouring stiff drinks and grilling up thick steaks since 1959. Since then, the area has gone through a major upswing—multimillion dollar homes, tech companies moving in. Everclear wrote that song. Through it all, this notorious dive has remained.

Literally steps away from the beach, Chez Jay has a more-than-

Chez Jay

friendly vibe—you'll feel like a regular on your first visit. Besides the good food—the Sand Dabs Sauté Almondine Chez Jay will knock your socks off—they also give away free peanuts. But not just any old peanuts. One of their peanuts traveled all the way to the moon in Alan Shepard's pocket. Jay calls it the first "Astro-nut." You can't make this up, folks.

YE RUSTIC INN

$$

1831 Hillhurst Avenue

LOS FELIZ

323-662-5757

yerusticinn.com

Ye Rustic Inn is the type of dark and dingy sports bar where hipsters go to drink PBR ironically and laugh at everyone who's not them. Metallica

Ye Rustic Inn

is usually blaring ironically from the ironic jukebox, but here's the thing: this place has the best wings on the East Side. Try the Atomic sauce. Don't fret—the servers are quick to refill your water glass.

The woodsy decor and rather large booths make this an ideal place to meet all your rowdy friends. But tell them to show up on time because this joint fills up fast. There's a decent happy hour with $5 beer and a shot (naturally), as well as sliders or fish tacos for only a few bucks. I recommend sticking to the Monday Night $25 Wing Special, which only lasts for a few hours (4–9 p.m.), but you get 12 wings and a pitcher of Budweiser for $25. If you can find a better deal on wings and beer, eat/drink it!

THE EDMON

$$$

5168 Melrose Avenue

LARCHMONT

323-645-5225

theedmon.com

My last trip here, I indulged in a plate of truffle steak fries, baby hot fried chicken drumbeats, mini lobster rolls, and a cucumber daiquiri. At these prices, I don't even care if my credit card's maxed—I'm eating like a king! Monarchs don't need to worry about money.

As such, I ordered up some dessert—one of each! Bread pudding with toasted honey meringue and white chocolate pearls; and a regal-looking banana split—vanilla and strawberry miso ice cream, chocolate ganache, and matcha white chocolate. Now I'm really eating like a king. At this rate, I may even develop gout. The disease of kings!

ESTERS WINE SHOP & BAR

$$

1314 7th Street

SANTA MONICA

310-899-6900

esterswineshop.com

I love wining and dining on or near the ocean. The air near seawater is supposedly loaded with electrolytes, which in theory makes you happier. And for whatever reason, there it is: I'm in a good mood again!

Or maybe it's because I'm dining on $15 half-dozen oysters and fancy-looking house cocktails. Or could it be that the vibe at Esters fosters a relaxed atmosphere? I guess we'll never know for sure. I'll have to keep coming back, week after week, until I get to bottom of this delicious mystery.

THE DRESDEN

$$$

1760 N Vermont Avenue

LOS FELIZ

323-665-4294

thedresden.com

Ten years ago, the Dresden was maybe the coolest bar in the city. You had Marty and Elayne jazzing it up most nights of the week, there were old-timers behind the bar who knew how to pour a gosh darn drink, and the vibe was very chill.

I'm still recommending this place because 1) The happy hour, with $2 off all cocktails and beer plus appetizers, is still a good deal. And the place is pretty quiet right at open, so you can have a relaxing drink. And 2) I'm a bit nostalgic sometimes. Marty and Elayne still play the hits like "Staying Alive" and "My Way," albeit a little slower and less frequently these days. All the old-timers have retired, replaced with mutants with man buns. But you know what? I look around, people are still having fun, talking about the industry, and getting a late-afternoon buzz. I'll go with the flow. Just a part of getting older, I guess. Maturity: It's a hell of a drug.

BACARI GDL

$$

757 Americana Way

GLENDALE

818-696-1460

bacarigdl.com

At some point, you should drop a bunch of money at the Glendale outdoor mall called the Americana. But after Gapping and J. Crewing for a few hours, you're probably gonna want a drink. Or five.

Bacari has one of the most insane happy hours I've ever heard of—for the measly price of $25 (less than a shirt at the Gap), they run an open bar. That is correct. Open. Bar. For the length of a Jennifer Aniston movie, you can have an endless stream of beer, wine, and sangria. That should help you forget all about the ugly clothes you just bought. Bottoms up!

GOOD TIMES AT DAVEY WAYNE'S

$$

1611 N El Centro Avenue

HOLLYWOOD

323-962-3804

goodtimesatdaveywaynes.com

This place is just straight-up dumb. That comes from a place of caring. Good Times at Davey Wayne's is like your dumb friend transmigrated into a brick-and-mortar bar in Hollywood. It's full of '70s kitsch such as ugly plaid couches and lava lamps, and people here like to have a rip-roaring good time (hence the name, probably). Happy hour beers go as low as 3 bucks, plus you can get an alcoholic sno-cone. Get the signature cocktail, the Davey's Old Fashioned. That's rye whiskey, angostura bitters, and orange and lemon peel oils. In the event all this rye and polyester has got you hungry, there's a food truck out back.

LAUREL POINT RESTAURANT

$$

12050 Ventura Boulevard

STUDIO CITY

818-769-6336

thepointseafood.com

Cruisin' for seafood in Studio City sounds like the worst Beach Boys song ever. The interior of Laurel Point was designed by the wizards at Kelly Architects, which gives the vibe of being inside a world-class ship—despite the fact that the restaurant is located in a strip mall. Their happy hour runs Monday through Friday, starting early at 3:30 p.m. and going until 6:30 p.m. Buck-fifty oysters are hard to beat, and the Blue Crab Dip with pimento cheese and jalapeños is divine.

I saw a couple ladies at the bar applaud their 47 Ronin cocktail, so you know it must be good. The wine selection is choice as well. So what are you waiting for? Hang a Gone Fishin' sign at your cubicle and get there before tide runs out. See what I did there? I hate myself.

FIG SANTA MONICA

$$$

101 Wilshire Boulevard

SANTA MONICA

310-319-3111

figsantamonica.com

FIG is a farm-to-table restaurant located inside the luscious Fairmont Hotel, a baseball's throw to the ocean. They have a wood-fire oven,

where they bake their own Bread Balloons (puffed-up lavash) as well as some out-of-this-world pizzas. FIG is also one of the very best happy hours in the city. I mean, duh, it's on the list.

While happy hour is seven days a week, the catch is that it only lasts *one hour.* So don't pussyfoot around. Most menu items are 50 percent off, and this includes an Albacore Tuna Crudo with fennel and aji amarillo, Spicy Fries with harissa powder, and Wood Roasted Beets. The Fig Burger is my go-to—always with a sunny-side up egg and baker's bacon added on top. FIG has their own fromager, or as I call him, the Head Cheese guy. His name is Eric Brazel and he personally picks all the cheese for the plates. You can even order something called Eric's Stash. I swear it won't get you in trouble with the police.

PLAN CHECK

$$

1111 Wilshire Boulevard

DTLA

213-403-1616

plancheck.com

Weekday nights in DTLA are certainly made better with the addition of Plan Check's happy hour. For starters, they have a variety of wines for only $5. Want a chicken or beef taco? Well, you're in luck, since they both cost a measly dollar. And they're served in the deep-fried shell that makes this former Midwestern fat kid feel right at home.

Plan Check also does their own style of sloppy joe, only this one is with chorizo chili. It's bonkers. I like to pair that sandwich with their Pastrami Gravy Fries.

Plan Check

One more heart-stopping menu item: Plan Check does a dynamite Cruller Donut, loaded with cream and slices of banana. It's almost too pretty to eat. *Almost.*

HINANO CAFE

$

15 Washington Boulevard

VENICE

310-822-3902

hinanocafevenice.com

Hinano Cafe, which isn't a cafe at all but Venice's best dive bar, serves up one of the better burgers on the West Side. Their weekly happy hour is a great place to quench your thirst after a day spent Rollerblading the Venice Boardwalk before heading back out to participate in the nightly drum circle. Opened in 1962, you can almost see the ghost of Jim Morrison hunched over in the corner, sucking down a Bud and scribbling down some lyrics.

The Venice Beach of today is far different than when Hinano came upon the scene. Every day I say a prayer that it can last another 50-plus years. But as you know, the future is uncertain and the end is always . . .

REDBIRD

$$$

114 E 2nd Street

DTLA

213-788-1191

redbird.la

After soaking in some art at MOCA or sunbathing at Pershing Square, make sure to stop in at chef Neal Fraser's flagship Redbird for their Modern American Cuisine. Happy hour lasts for just one hour after

opening, but there are great deals on seasonal small and large plates meant for a gathering of friends.

The wine list focuses on Burgundy, Bordeaux, and California—which is kind of like the Hamilton, Joe Frank, and Reynolds of fine wine.

I really love the Chicken Pot Pie, where the gravy is thick like chowder. They even put pieces of chicken hearts in there. And I shouldn't have to clue you in on the crispy Sweetbreads with preserved lemon, black garlic (!), and radish salad. I'm also really into the Shishito Peppers and crispy quinoa, washed down with a mint julep. As a fan, I particularly appreciate the nods to horse racing on the cocktail menu, with such drinks as the Preakness (rye, cognac, sweet vermouth, Bénédictine, and bitters) and the Belmont Breeze (bourbon, amontillado sherry, lemon, and grenadine).

CECCONI'S

$$$

8764 Melrose Avenue

 WEST HOLLYWOOD

310-432-2000

cecconiswesthollywood.com

Want to unwind at a modern-day classic Italian restaurant? One that serves a knockout black truffle cheeseburger, not to mention all of the handmade pastas and pizzetta? Then get yourself to Cecconi's in West Hollywood.

The happy hour runs from 4 to 7 p.m., but I suggest showing up a few minutes earlier. The bar tends to fill up fast, and they don't serve happy hour in the dining room. Once seated, order the aforementioned Black Truffle Burger. This standout, not available on the regular menu, comes with Fontina cheese and pancetta, served on a toasted brioche bun. Did I mention it's four lousy bucks? Crazy, right? The happy hour wine list consists of a house rosé from France, a chardonnay from Italy, and a pinot noir from Germany. They'll also happily make you a margarita on the rocks. At an Italian restaurant? Why not? The globalists won a long time ago, my friend.

SHOO SHOO BABY

$$

717 W 7th Street

213-688-7755

shoobabyla.com

There aren't many bars that feature a manifesto on their homepage explaining that they believe in the power of femininity, and that all bars shouldn't cater to the bros and dudes of the world, and that texting at the table (or bar) is lame. But this one does—and kudos to them.

I went ten whole minutes before texting about how gorgeous the interior of Shoo Shoo Baby was and how the service was friendly— even though they were shaking their heads at me. But then my friends arrived and we got down to serious business: drinking and eating cheese. Someone in my party ordered the Piss 'n Vinegar, which is

Shoo Shoo Baby

Shoo Shoo Baby

Pierda Almas mezcal, jalapeño, agave syrup, pineapple spritz, and a splash of sparkling wine, served on the rocks with a lemon twist. I snacked on charcuterie plate that included Tartufo salami (imbued with black Italian truffles!) and a mild, nutty sheep's milk cheese, Petit Basque. Another friend tossed back a glass of Dhondt-Grellet

Champagne. We all laughed, avoided texting, neglected Twitter, sent zero snaps. FOMO be gone!

THE HUDSON

$$

1114 N Crescent Heights Boulevard

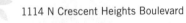

WEST HOLLYWOOD

323-654-6686

thehudsonla.com

You know West Hollywood's the Hudson is trendy by the name of their happy hour—which they call the Huddy Hour. By next year, it'll be called Hud Hr—mark my words. It's like when my favorite store in the mall, Pacific Sunwear, simplified and became Pac Sun. Whenever I ask a millennial where Pacific Sunwear is, they give me this look like I'm a real dummy.

So when I got into my Uber and told my driver to take me to Huddy Hour, he knew *exactly* where to take me. This is a place where you can get four-buck cocktails, or upgrade to a specialty one for two Washingtons more. There's also a bunch of small-plate menu items for $7. Your best bet is either the short rib tacos (that chipotle crema tho) or the Mac & Cheese with smoked jalapeño, parmesan bread crumbs, shallots, and garlic. After rubbing my full belly, I snagged another Uber, went home, and ordered a new pair of joggers from Pac Sun.

BRACK SHOP TAVERN

$$

525 W 7th Street

DTLA

213-232-8657

brackshoptavern.com

I love sports. Probably too much, if there's such a thing. Many's the night when I can't think of a better way to spend an evening than with some

good grub and an ice-cold nonalcoholic beer watching "a bunch of pituitary cases try to stuff a ball through a hoop," as Alvy Singer's girlfriend might say. Brack Shop Tavern in DTLA is one of the few places in that area where a guy like me can unselfconsciously and cheaply hang out. There are plenty of TVs, beer, and cocktails in the $4 to $6 range, as well as corn dogs. Lemme repeat that last part. *Corn. Dogs.* If you didn't drop your copy of this book and head there right now, then I don't know what's going to become of you. Nothing good, probably. The mole tacos are also a treat. Plus, Brack Shop has a game room complete with an N-64! Have I ever told you the story of how I was an expert-level Goldeneye-for-N-64 player? And that I won a college tournament with a cash prize of $25? My friends and I ate well that week. But not as well as if Brack Shop Tavern had been in my life all those beers ago.

BEST BREWERIES

Over the last few years, LA has seen a boom in independent breweries. Here's a list of some of the best places to help grow your (not so) micro beer belly!

10. Highland Park Brewery (Highland Park)

9. Boomtown Brewery (DTLA)

8. Golden Road Brewing (Glendale)

7. Macleod Ale Brewing (Van Nuys)

6. Arts District Brewing (Arts District)

5. Smog City (Torrance)

4. Eagle Rock Brewery (Eagle Rock)

3. Mumford Brewing (Little Tokyo)

2. Craftsman Brewing (Pasadena)

1. Modern Times (DTLA)

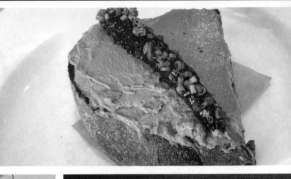

4

CULINARY HEROES (DINNER)

"Good food is a benign weapon against the sodden way we live."

—Jim Harrison

What makes a restaurant an ideal place for dinner? Obviously, food plays a major factor. But it's not the only component. Ambience, the architecture of a building, the wine list, friendliness of the waitstaff, type of music, the soft lighting at the bar—each little detail helps in creating the ultimate eating experience.

I've compiled a list of my favorite spots for dinner. Some of the places below are super fancy; others need no reservation nor have any sort of strict dress code. There's a bit of everything—steak houses, Thai dynamos, Neo-Mediterranean, and more. Whatever you're possibly in the mood for can be found here.

When reading this list, you will begin to notice how much the personality of the executive chef at a particular restaurant plays into shaping the overall experience. Some chefs, you will learn, handpick the specific music that customers will hear, or help in the layout of the dining room. These are men and women who are completely obsessed with providing a unique, memorable event, which is good news for you!

CASSIA

$$$

1314 7th Street

SANTA MONICA

310-393-6699

cassiala.com

Celebrating the dynamic flavors of southeast Asia mixed with a certain homegrown California vibe, including ingredients sourced by their very own farmers, Cassia—a duo of husband and wife duos (it sounds weird but it makes sense if you read it three times, I promise)—reigns supreme in Santa Monica. With its laid-back vibe and abundance of natural light, this is a perfect place to grab a drink and some oysters at the bar.

There's a considerable patio section as well, with long, communal tables that are superb for group meals. An added bonus: You don't need a reservation for the patio, which is great since the dining room is often packed open-to-close. For the table, try a southeast Asian-inspired charcuterie plate, with salted pork and grilled bread, Vietnamese meatloaf, and smoked red sausage. From the appetizers menu, order the Grilled Pig's Tail that looks more charred than grilled, but the fat of the meat is soft and is meant to be dipped into a fish sauce for maximum salty flavor. Eventually, move on to the Whole Grilled Sea Bass with turmeric, dill, and lime, and perfectly crispy skin.

Or you can go with the Vietnamese Pot Au Feu. This is a short rib stew with potatoes, cabbage, carrots, bone marrow, bird's eye chile sauce, and walnut mustard. Grilled bread is provided for sopping up all that broth.

On to dessert: I prefer the Kaffir Lime Custard, an insanely rich custard topped with lychee whipped cream and chocolate mint. Somebody more knowledgeable about wine than I am will clue you in on their extensive selection, comprising some 80 bottles spanning Europe before settling back into familiar Cali terroir. Cassia is a most welcoming dinner destination, be it a routine after-work celebration (didn't get fired!) or, you know, you managed a second date. Either way, things are looking up for you.

ROSSOBLU

$$$

1124 San Julian Street

DTLA

213-749-1099

rossoblula.com

Chef Steve Samson's mammoth open-space joint, located in the Fashion District of DTLA, is a true family affair. After leaving Sotto, Samson and his wife Dina decided to create the ultimate Italian restaurant. The menu is an expert take on the cuisine from the northern Italian region of Emilia Romagna, or as Samson might remember it, where his grandparents lived. Many of the selections are a direct homage to the dishes he grew up with, recipes passed down from the older generation.

For starters, try the Grilled Morro Bay Oysters, cooked in brown butter, lemon, and bread crumbs—a delectable mix of sea-saltiness and buttery savor. Another must-have is the Braised Pork Meatballs served on grilled polenta bread. I also enjoy the Swiss Chard Erbazzone Tartlet, with chicory salad and Stacchino cheese.

The true stars of the menu, however, are the pastas; like Mom's Minestra Nel Sacco, wrapped up Parmigiano Reggiano dumplings, served in a chicken broth. The ricotta-filled Tortelloni comes bathed in butter, with sprinkles of Parmigiano Reggiano. But perhaps the standout dish is the delicate, forest green Pappardelle noodles, with sausage ragu, broccoli, and ricotta crema. This is the dish you keep coming back for, over and over again. Foodies of LA are deeply indebted to chef Samson's nonna e nonno.

SPAGO

$$$$

176 N Canon Drive

 BEVERLY HILLS

310-385-0880

wolfgangpuck.com/dining/spago

Undoubtedly, if you are of a certain age—which I am not—you have heard of Spago without ever having stepped foot into LA. In its day, it was as famous as a brick-and-mortar eatery could be. You could spot pictures of the place in *People* Magazine or on the news. Wolfgang Puck's flagship Beverly Hills restaurant, for a considerable run of time, was *the* place for celebrities to mingle with dignitaries, and where the very idea of New California Cuisine was invented.

While its star-power has dimmed ever so slightly, Spago still offers up a spectacular tasting menu. For *only* $145, the California Tasting Menu is a 13-course journey through each of Wolfgang's most acclaimed creations. Just a brief sample: the now-legendary Spicy Tuna Tartare in a sesame-miso cone cup; the Egg, which is in fact a smoked salmon mousse, Weiser Farm's Potato Chip, Espuma, and Salmon pearls; Lacquered Carpenter's Ranch Squab, a Szechuan pepper "rock," soy powder "twigs," and red sorrel; Maine Lobster in Charred Onion "Bowl"; and finally, the Chocolate Crepe Soufflé, topped with salted caramel whipped cream.★

Spago offers a regular dining menu as well. Start your night off with the Spanish Octopus (coincidentally, my nickname in high school). Housed inside a young coconut, the octopus comes charred with a habanero kick. I also devoured the Kabocha Squash Soup, served with a parmesan crisp. On to the main course, might you try the Grilled Lamb Rack, with falafel "macarons" and smoky eggplant caviar. The marinated lamb is grilled to a perfect rare temperature—oh-so-juicy and tender.

If you really feel like making it rain, then go with the True A-5 Japanese Wagyu New York Steak. Wagyu is one of the highest-grade cuts of beef on the planet, hailing from Japanese cows. Isn't it odd that something can be both Japanese AND New York? Where else could you describe something like that? I guess that *Godzilla* remake starring Matthew Broderick I saw in high school (the night I got that nickname). This steak is much, MUCH better than that movie.

What's really cool about Spago is that on any given night, there's a mighty good chance you'll see Mr. Puck himself making his way through the dining area, talking with customers, posing for pictures. Heck, Matthew Broderick might even be there. He'll take a picture with you. Just don't tell him what I said about his movie.

—————————

* Mr. Puck likes to change things up by rotating the menu every few months or years. So if something described here isn't on the menu when you visit, please don't sue me. Don't sue Mr. Puck either. He has better lawyers than you do.

ANIMAL

$$$

435 N Fairfax Avenue

FAIRFAX

323-782-9225

animalrestaurant.com

Food historians will one day describe Jon Shook and Vinny Dotolo's flagship restaurant Animal as the Big Bang in high-scale-yet-casual dining.

Closing in on a decade of existence, Animal still delivers an exciting menu, with such offerings as the exuberantly rich Poutine with oxtail

Animal

gravy and Cheddar; Veal Tongue; and Sweetbreads on top of creamed spinach, hen of the woods, caper, and brown butter.

The intimate, sparsely decorated space and mood lighting create an ideal date night. Share a bite of the Chicken Liver Toast—perhaps the best in town. My personal favorite is the Pig Ear, which tastes not unlike bacon and comes with a masterfully cooked over-easy egg and a spicy citrus sauce. Not sure if this counts as breakfast for dinner—I do know this is better than anything they serve at Waffle House. Or go wild for the foie gras terrine with orange marmalade and satsuma.

Bone marrow dishes have been the flavor of the month for many months now, and Animal does a darn good one. Theirs comes broiled with chimichurri and caramelized onions.

I'm sure you noticed the lack of vegetarian dishes mentioned. Well, what would you expect from a place called Animal? They do have a few options, though. The gem lettuce, beet, and feta plate looks both colorful and yummy. But tbh, I come here to live out my caveman fantasies, minus the hunting and gathering part. Just the eating part. Don't even think of doing any paintings on the wall, either. They'll kick you out.

Despite being around for more than a decade, you still need a reservation if you wanna get a seat here. If waiting isn't your style, you can always grab a seat at the bar, which serves beer and wine only.

Finally, if you don't save enough room for dessert and try the Bacon Chocolate Crunch Bar with salt and pepper ice cream, you're dead to me!

A.O.C

$$$

8700 W 3rd Street

BEVERLY GROVE

310-859-9859

aocwinebar.com

By combining local cuisine with a stylish and stylized European influence, chef Suzanne Goin and sommelier Caroline Styne's fine dining

A.O.C.

A.O.C.

establishment A.O.C. has been garnering praise and packing seats since 2002. Early adapters of cured meats and small plates, A.O.C. won over many an Angeleno by tapping into flavors from Italy, Spain, and North Africa. After changing locations in 2012 to a much bigger and more dapper spot, A.O.C. is also one of the most gorgeous restaurants featured in this book. A true masterpiece of design, it features an intimate dining room as well as a majestic outdoor patio, which somehow manages to muffle the street sounds of this otherwise busy neighborhood. Both are ideal for date night. It's like stepping inside a brochure for a holiday you can take any night of the week. So it should go without saying that getting a reservation is key. You can even book the wine room for a private dining experience. Overlooking the garden patio, this wood-paneled den allows you to take a gander at their mucho impressive wine collection. And it seats about 40 people, which is perfect if you own an NFL team.

Let's talk about the menu. Specifically, the Spanish Fried Chicken. A crispy piece of chicken tender served with romesco aioli and chili-cumin butter, it's one of the most flavorful bites you'll ever experience. I also recommend the Grilled Whole Fish (rotating) with preserved lemon labneh. A.O.C. is a great spot for you vegetarians, too. Tell the always friendly waiter you'll have the fingerling potatoes with crème fraîche and chives. He or she will probably nod and say, "Excellent choice." Because it *is* an excellent choice. And you're welcome. A.O.C. also features offerings from their wood oven such as the Wood-Roasted Shrimp with parsley aioli; or clams, doused in sherry and green garlic, and served with toast. Marvelous!

The bar is led by Christiaan Rollich, who excels at meticulously crafted cocktails. Unwind with a Sancho Panza—vodka with ginger beer, lemon, and sherry. Just make sure to have a designated donkey to take you home.

Eating with friends? Then cap off a wonderful night with A.O.C.'s Dessert Platter: vanilla pot de crème with Spanish chocolate and marcona almonds, chocolate torta with coffee cream, and an assortment of house-made chocolates, candied nuts, and confections. Or gorge on the whole thing yourself. Be somebody, baby.

MAMA LION

$$

601 S Western Avenue

KOREATOWN

213-377-5277

mamalion.com

This Koreatown supper club is the return of acclaimed chef Michael Hung. The contemporary, California-style menu of shared plates, raw bar selections, and inspired entrees can be enjoyed while sitting at the central bar, sipping cocktails and people gazing. The Kelly Architects-designed interior features an industrial-style exposed brick wall and leather seating, as well as a heavenly glow from hanging chandeliers. The aforementioned cocktails are overseen by Aidan Demarest, who made his name at Spare Room and Seven Grand.

So what to eat? Well, for starters, it should be noted that Mama Lion offers caviar service. There are also oysters on the half shell and yellowtail crudo. For shared appetizers, try the seared foie gras, accompanied by grilled brioche and watercress.

Mama Lion is doing their share to perpetuate the fast-growing, newly chic Koreatown vibe by asking customers to "dress to impress." This means my "Single and Ready to Mingle" shirt and jhorts won't cut it. Luckily, the shirt fits rather snugly, so I can wear it under my tux.

KISMET

$$

4648 Hollywood Boulevard

LOS FELIZ

323-409-0404

kismetlosangeles.com

Kismet

Kismet has rebooted the notion of Middle Eastern flavors for the modern California eater. The food comes served family-style, a notion usually reserved for places like Ponderosa and Olive Garden, so bring family, or at least coworkers you can stomach being around. Former New Yorker Sara Kramer and Chicago native Sarah Hymanson use locally sourced ingredients to create their small-plate wonders. The vibe at Kismet is neighborly, embodied by their chummy yet attentive waitstaff.

For starters, I recommend the freekeh fritters, with their perfect dip-friendly pickle green sauce. The spiced cashews with kaffir lime leaf are also quite a treat. Main dishes of note include the potatoes with labneh, macadamia nuts, cured scallop, and urfa pepper, which is utterly comforting in its creamy textures. Also try the manila clams with tomatoes, butter beans, and spinach.

Or, as you will notice on the menu, you could go big and order the

Kismet

Rabbit for Two. So I guess that means you and somebody will go big. Or go home. But you can't go home till you've had the Mahleb Ice Cream with mulberry and strawberry compote and crystallized honey. Hands down one of the best desserts in the city.

BESTIA

$$$

2121 E 7th Place

ARTS DISTRICT

213-514-5724

bestiala.com

Located in the most industrial part of the Arts District (seriously, the exterior looks like a meat-packing plant), Bestia still reigns as one of the go-to destinations in the city. And for good reason! Besides the stellar menu and drinks, the atmosphere here is alive, maybe due in part to the bouncy sound from the open concrete walls and floors.

Bestia still feels like a well-kept secret. Here, you'll find some of the best pastas around: the Tagliatelle al Sugo di Maiale, which is a pork ragu, house-made speck, baby kale, and caraway seeds. Or give the Spaghetti Rustichella with Dungeness crab a try. Both are completely irresistible. Not enough? Very well, then. They serve a Roasted Marrow Bone that is out of this world—perfectly seasoned, buttery, and complemented nicely with a melt-in-your-mouth spinach gnocchetti.

Afterward, you can live la vita dolce with their mind-boggling dessert menu. For my money (or yours, which I'd be happy to spend), the Crème Fraîche Panna Cotta with mara des bois strawberries, blood orange honey syrup, and whole-wheat butter cookies is where it's at.

You'll have one of the Best(ia) nights ever!

CONNIE & TED'S

$$$

8171 Santa Monica Boulevard

323-848-2722

connieandteds.com

Chef Michael Cimarusti chose to name his seafood restaurant after his grandparents: Ted, a former Navy man, was a devoted East seaboard fisherman; his wife Connie grilled up that afternoon's catch. Now partnering with Executive Chef Sam Baxter, Cimarusti is firm in the belief that seafood needs only the lightest touch, the simplest preparation. The catch at Connie & Ted's is undeniably fresh, from the raw oysters and clams to the chilled Wild White American Shrimp or Topnecks—all of which pair perfectly with an ice-cold beer at the bar.

There's the trio of distinctive Chowders (dubbed Jo's Wicked Good Chowda')—the creamy New England, the ruby-red Manhattan, and the salty Rhode Island. Some fella named Ed has a Portuguese Fish Stew named after him featuring the catch of the day, clams, mussels, and linquiça. You'll feel like you settled in Boston Harbor with the Lobster Roll sandwich, either served hot with drawn butter (!) or cold with mayonnaise (also !). And finally, for dessert, a Blondie with vanilla ice cream and caramel sauce. It's just like being on a boat out in the middle of the Atlantic. Minus the seasickness.

ELF CAFE

$$

2135 Sunset Boulevard

ECHO PARK

213-484-6829

elfcafe.com

You don't have to be a vegetarian to marvel at the meatless wonders on the menu of Echo Park's impishly delightful Elf Cafe. This place is a testament to the beauty of nature. The flora-heavy dining room is a botanist's dream—you won't know where the wall ends and your plate begins! Chef Dave Martinez has developed a distinctly modern take on Mediterranean classics, including the Classic Spicy Kale salad, with green charmoula, harissa, avocado, seeds, and feta. Another standout is the Greek Risotto. This work of art features heirloom zucchini (!), market greens, and Aegean sheep cheese. You won't find better sheep cheese anywhere—unless you're a herder in Crete.

There's the Crispy Potato Cutlet with Roasted Cauliflower and herbed labneh (you can substitute a vegan yogurt). On the main course side, there's the Pasta Carbonara with Maitake Mushrooms. To quote the great Jimmy Walker—it's Dyno-mite!

Elf also prides itself on serving only natural, sustainable wines. Check out their website for Joseph Harper's personal selections.

MAUDE

$$$$

212 S Beverly Drive

BEVERLY HILLS

310-859-3418

mauderestaurant.com

Since opening in 2014, chef Curtis Stone's culinary tribute to his grandmother has retained all the intimacy of a family meal. The set nine-course tasting menu is centered around a seasonal ingredient, selected anew each month, which is expertly woven into each course and creates a harmonious eating experience.

The dining room is small (7 tables), rustic in appearance, and reservations can be hard to come by. To say the least. And four guests is the maximum size party they allow—so think about who you really want to bring along. The food is served on china adorned with gaudy flower patterns seemingly picked up from the Fairfax Flea Market—it's

clear Stone obsesses over each and every detail. He is chef-as-auteur, and
Maude is his masterpiece.

PINE & CRANE

$$

1521 Griffith Park Boulevard

SILVER LAKE

323-668-1128

pineandcrane.com

Growing up in the Midwest meant Chinese food came (usually within
30 minutes) in white boxes with red Mandarin characters, chopsticks
never used, and a fortune cookie to close out the meal. Can't forget
the leftovers. Cold white rice with gelatinized "orange" sauce for
breakfast!

Pine & Crane aims to serve fast-casual Chinese food, but made from
ingredients sourced from a local family farm. This is Silver Lake, after
all—not the Midwest. The Minced Pork on Rice, with soy-braised
egg, rice, and house daikon pickle is a bowl of complete satisfaction.
Embrace the Dan Dan Noodles: sesame peanut sauce, chili oil,
cucumbers, and peanuts. And don't forget to order a side of Panfried
Pork Buns, a Cantonese staple. Possibly the best you'll have outside of
the Mainland.

RUEN PAIR

$

5257 Hollywood Boulevard

LOS FELIZ

323-466-0153

ruenpairthaila.com

Located on the edge of Los Feliz and, you guessed it, Thai Town, Ruen
Pair is the Thai restaurant for those of us completely enamored with

Thai food. My dish of choice is the BBQ Pork over Rice, a lip-smacking combo of BBQ pork and Chinese sausages, with a boiled egg over rice and gravy sauce. Make sure to get extra chili sauce. Another standout is the Tom Yum Goonng. This spicy soup is served with buoyant pieces of shrimp, mushrooms, lemongrass, a squirt of lime juice, and fresh chili. Yum Tom indeed, Tom! (Who's Tom? Are you Tom?)

Sometimes at a restaurant, I like to order something just to say that I ordered it. You know, to show off to friends what an adventurous eater I've become. At Ruen Pair, that item is the Duck Feet Salad. Duck Feet! No, there won't be a pair of webbed feet sticking out of the bowl. The feet are diced small and tossed with rice, red onion, chili, and lime juice. It's actually delicious.

Ruen Pair is quick and casual, so no need for a reservation. And they're still cash only. FYI, they also stay open as late as 3 a.m., just in case you get a hankerin' for duck feet in the middle of the night.

BEST POKÉ

Ever scroll through your Instagram feed and see a friend or two extol the wonders of the poké bowl? Did you ask yourself, "What's poké?" Just so you're not left in the lurch, poké is, like, sushi 2.0. But way easier to eat! Now stop wasting time and get to these spots, slow-poké.

10. PokiNometry (Hollywood)

9. Ohana Poké Co. (Silver Lake)

8. Poké N Roll Sushi (Glendale)

7. Wiki Poké (Koreatown)

6. Sweetfin Poké (Silver Lake)

5. Poké Me (Westwood)

4. Mainland Poké (West Hollywood)

3. Pokémolé (Westlake)

2. Okipoki (DTLA)

1. Poké-Poké (Venice)

SILVERLAKE RAMEN

$

2927 Sunset Boulevard

SILVER LAKE

323-660-8100

silverlakeramen.com

There will be a wait. Just want to be up front with you. This place, located right in the middle of Hipsterville (a.k.a. Silver Lake), always has a line out the door. For good reason: The ramen is on point.

My go-to bowl is the Spicy Tonkotsu Ramen. The spice of this broth will definitely warm even the coldest heart. Not that I'm saying you have a cold heart. You seem lovely. Treat yourself and top it off with a slice of pork belly. You've earned it.

Not into spicy broth? Then the Mazemen is calling your name. This bowl comes filled with ground pork, chives, seaweed, and poached egg.

Silverlake Ramen

Personally, I like to sit at the noodle bar. From there, I can watch the talented chefs dice chilis, poach eggs, or roll sushi. Oh yeah, and this place does a mean Crispy Rice with Spicy Tuna roll.

If you'd rather take it and go, make sure you call ahead or place your order online. Like I mentioned earlier, this place is happening, so beat the rush. Time is money, or so I've read.

ROSALINÉ

$$$

8479 Melrose Avenue

323-297-9500

rosalinela.com

Chef Ricardo Zarate's Rosaliné transplants classic Peruvian street food into a more formal, West Hollywood environment, beautifully presenting and preserving the core flavors of his youth. Dishes are designed to be shared here, so go with a group of friends. Pass around a plate of the Corazon Anticucho, beef heart skewers with rustic rocoto peppers, feta cheese, and walnut sauce. Another keystone dish is the crispy Chicharron de Paiche. This is served with popped kiwicha (a Peruvian super-seed—minus the flapping cape), fried paiche (freshwater fish found in the Amazon—the jungle, not the supplier), and yuzu aioli sauce. To quote the late, great Peruvian political writer César Vallejo, "It's delicious!"

From their La Familia, or family-style dishes, the Chaufa Paella was a big hit with people I brought, who—just to be straight with you—were not my family. The paella has Peruvian fried rice, pancetta, la chang sausage, and prawns. The little sausage bites are scrumptious, while the whole plate has a hint of ginger freshness to it. For dessert, my non-family members and I shared the fun-to-say Bon Bon Bons! Lucuma (!) ice cream, chocolate ice cream, and strawberry mint sorbet, each dipped in a Peruvian chocolate. As a guy who isn't my brother said when he took a bite, "Good Lawd!" I tend to agree.

ALIMENTO

$$$

1710 Silver Lake Boulevard

SILVER LAKE

323-928-2888

alimentola.com

If you aren't paying close attention, or don't have friends who have been here and raved about this place, Alimento can be sort of easy to miss. Tucked away between overpriced handbag stores and other trust-funded knickknack boutiques, and across from the music venue, the Satellite, a simple neon sign labeled only with an A sits above the door to this soulful Italian eatery.

Alimento has a bustling atmosphere—occasionally the dining room is a bit too loud. Recent adjustments, including adding noise-absorbing wall mounts, have helped. And the decor is minimalistic, at best. The food, however . . .

Chef Zach Pollack has created exciting new takes on old favorites. For example, their version of Pig in a Blanket: mortadella, spelt pastry, brovada, and stracchino. It's a big block of utter goodness. Their chicken liver crostone is beautifully textured and for balance comes with a cooling sweet plum jam. Another stellar dish is the Tortellini in Brodo. The pasta is cooked perfectly al dente, each bite a buttery, cheese-suffused delight. The plate looks so pretty you might hesitate digging in, unsure if this is meant to be eaten or hung at LACMA.

CUGURT

$

1904 Hillhurst Avenue

LOS FELIZ

323-486-7022

cugurt.com

This quaint Persian-Greek hybrid has been a Los Feliz go-to since the late '90s when it was known as El Greco. Now moved a street over, and with a new, sorta confusing name, Cugurt is home to some of the best gyros and lamb plates outside of the Parthenon. There's also a handful of healthy versions, including the couscous meal. A big ol' bowl of tomatoes, greens, cucumbers, avocado, and feta cheese—not to mention the couscous. Throw in some lamb meat from a rotating spit and you're all set.

The only thing I don't get is that name. Was "Yocumber" already taken? Guess "White Sauce" isn't exactly appetizing either. But what do I know?

NIGHT + MARKET SONG

$$

3322 W Sunset Boulevard

SILVER LAKE

323-665-5899

nightmarketsong.com

Gwyneth Paltrow counts herself as one of the great admirers of chef Kris Yenbamroong's Night + Market restaurants (there's also the original in WeHo). Maybe it's the funky decor—hot, Barbie pink exterior; interior consisting of lava lamp orange walls, an inexplicable Cindy Crawford poster, and a Michael Jackson shrine in the men's room. It's normal if your first impression of the place is "WTF?" But you'll soon come to appreciate its quirks.

And the menu, too, can, at first glance, seem a little off-putting. I mean, they do serve *luu suk*, otherwise known as Blood Soup. Blood. Soup. I'm sure it's delicious (I'm not *that* adventurous), but there are definitely some choice menu items for your delectation.

Most famous is the Fried Chicken Sandwich. They boast about its notoriety on the outside wall. A crunchy, chiengrai-style fried chicken thigh, with a papaya slaw, and ranch dressing for a cooling balance. It's both unique and somehow very familiar. Most important, it's dang good. Another hit dish is the Fried Lamb "Meatballs" made of pork, pork liver, and blood. It's a big plate of garlicky goodness. If Night + Market Song looks like it's a Thai version of that '80s-themed restaurant in *Back to the Future II*, it's probably because Yenbamroong is a film school graduate.

From building to plate, everything is visually pleasing. Even, I must admit, the Blood Soup.

PALERMO

$$

1858 N Vermont Avenue

 LOS FELIZ

323-663-1178

palermoristoranteitaliano.com

Palermo is a classic neighborhood Italian restaurant. It's been *my* neighborhood pizza place for nearly a decade. I love the people who work here: Tony, the owner, is as friendly as they come. The food ain't fancy—

Palermo

and I mean that as a compliment. There's no deconstructed pasta dishes here. You order spaghetti and meatballs, by gum, that's what you're gonna get.

Which is fine by me. Sometimes all I crave is down-home comfort food. And if that comes in the shape of a pizza, all the better. Palermo specializes in a Pizzarosa-style pie. A rich, sweet tomato-based sauce with a blanket of briny feta, shoelace stringy mozzarella, and a nutty Parmigiano on a thick, slightly over-baked bread. You can go with the medium size since you'll most likely be stuffed after two slices.

Pro tip: This pizza is even more rad cold the next day. Plus, you wanna leave a little room for one of their house-made cannoli, paired perfectly with a frothy cappuccino.

SUMMER BUFFALO

$$

7275 Melrose Avenue

FAIRFAX

323-938-8808

summerbuffalo.com

Summer Buffalo can be expensive. Not the food or drinks, mind you. Those are all reasonably priced. And delicious, too. Especially the Tom Yum soup. Served with chicken, this spicy sour soup warms the cockles of my heart. Both literally and figuratively. It's got a real nice kick to it. Prefer something a bit cooler? Then the Tom Kah soup is for you. It's the same setup as the Yum but with coconut milk. For the entrée, order up some Not-So-Ordinary Orange Chicken. Served with sticky white rice, it always manages to be both crispy and tender. Speaking of sticky rice . . . their dessert Mango & Sticky Rice is a must-close to every meal.

So where does the expensive part come in? It seems that without fail, every time I finish a meal at Summer Buffalo, I start to look up flights to Thailand. Maybe I could spend some time there, soak up some sun, spices, and, best of all, I hear you can pet a wild monkey. But after checking my bank account, I realize my money (what little I have) is

Summer Buffalo

better spent eating here. Summer Buffalo is close enough to the real thing. Minus the monkey.

FELIX TRATTORIA

$$$

1023 Abbot Kinney Boulevard

VENICE

424-387-8622

felixla.com

Chef Evan Funke has been described as a "culinary storyteller." Indeed, he has quite a story—at the very least, a pedigreed history—to share: he was the head chef at the beloved Mediterranean small-plate diner, Rustic Canyon, then moved on to run his own porchetta truck. Now he finds himself near the beach, taking his passion for painstakingly handcrafted pasta dishes to Felix. You can watch him perform in an enclosed glass room, rolling out large sheets of pasta and tossing flour on them before allowing them to dry out.

Felix also serves top-notch pizzas. Order their Funghi pie, or mushroom pizza for the layperson. This pie comes with a bunch of stuff I had to look up in the dictionary! Like: Crescenza (Italian cow cheese) and Taleggio (a very soft cheese). Basically I learned I'm no fromager (somebody who knows their cheese).

For refreshments, go with the Too Soon? libation: gin, amaro, lemon, and orange. Cap the night off with a tantalizing piece of the tiramisu.

Oh, and make sure to get a picture of the #fuckyourpastamachine sign located on the wall of the pasta room. Post it to your Instagram and your followers will have FOMO in no time.

71ABOVE

$$$$

633 W 5th Street, 71st Floor

DTLA

213-712-2683

71above.com

Located 950 feet above ground level—just letting you know, in case you suffer from acrophobia—71Above offers possibly the most amazing view of any place listed in this book. You can see for miles and miles: a glimpse of Malibu from one side, the mountains on the other. It's breathtaking, frankly.

So the first thing you have to decide when deciding to dine at 71Above is which type of 71Above dining experience you want.

You can choose to dine at the bar, a most lively spot. You can order the full menu if you desire. Or there's the regular old dining room. You know the drill. You can choose to do the Chef's Table experience. This is a tad more refined, with a full view of the open kitchen. Next up are the semi-private and private dining options. All depends on how intimate you wanna get, or if you want a blimp's-eye perspective of Dodger Stadium.

71Above

And, of course, how much you feel like spending. Full disclosure, however you plan on dining, it's pricey, so don't forget the Diners Club card.

The menu is broken down into three courses. Off the starter list, there's fresh oysters, packed with champagne. That's class, baby! Follow it with the seared, strong-tasting Foie Gras with cocoa nibs and pink peppercorns. For the third course, get the Young Chicken, a full roasted breast with porcini and king oyster mushrooms, and a touch of black truffle, and a jus gras sauce rendered from the chicken fat. The dessert menu changes on the reg, but past hits such as the Crème Fraîche Mousse with hints of grapefruit or the Caramel Custard show they have the game down pat.

PREUX & PROPER

$$

840 S Spring Street

DTLA

213-896-0090

preuxandproper.com

Preux & Proper is bringing a decidedly bold take on Creole and Cajun cooking to DTLA. As the name might suggest, this place is split into two sections: the bar (Preux) and the, um, proper dining room (Proper). In honor of my past debauchery, I often choose the bar side.

The grub here is classic Southern comfort food, like the Turkey Neck Gravy Poutine, with collards on top of skin-on freedom fries; or the Fried Mississippi Catfish, with red remoulade sauce and house pickles. Oh, boy, there's also the po'boys! How does Fried Black Tiger Prawns grab ya? Dip that baby in their chunky cocktail sauce, which will undoubtedly land on the napkin you didn't forget to tuck into your shirt.

If you venture upstairs for a more formal setting, you can catch those prawns in a gumbo; order extra bread for sopping. There's also the Fried Whole Game Hen, with buttermilk biscuits, serrano jelly, and crushed pecans, perfectly gamey and sweet. Speaking of sweet, dessert is served on both levels, which means you have no excuse not to get Kassady's Mama's Key Lime Pie. Perhaps the best Key Lime in the city.

THE MAR VISTA

$$

12249 Venice Boulevard

VENICE

310-751-6773

themarvista.com

Chef Brandon Walker (a.k.a. Chef D) is staking his claim in that as-yet-unnamed section of town between Venice and Culver City, serving

"Progressive American Cuisine," with dishes that range from Colorado Leg of Lamb to Wild Boar Ragout & Penne Pasta. Seafood varieties include Oysters, New Zealand Rock Cod Ceviche, and Diver Scallops. Much of the produce is sourced from a community garden only a few blocks away.

The space—built and designed by John Reed of Reed Architecture and designer Gregory Swanson, respectively—feels like a large communal mess hall, with soft lighting and wooden beams above. It tends to get pretty lively during weekend nights, and features live music and a late-supper menu. The bar has a fairly decent selection of largely French and California wines. On the sweets side, there's the Scotch Kiss Brownie Bites with salted caramel, coco crisps, and marshmallows. Sound progressive enough? I think so, too.

SWEET CHICK

$$

448 N Fairfax Avenue

 FAIRFAX

323-592-3423

sweetchick.com

By way of that hipster haven known as Brooklyn, Sweet Chick is now located in the Fairfax District, propagating their dogmatic belief in damn good fried chicken and waffles, experimental cocktails, and a giddy, childlike vibe. And by that I mean, you can get drunk while eating yummy chicken and bacon-Cheddar waffles. Or Mac and Cheese loaded with Gruyere, Fontina, aged white Cheddar, and, for crunch, crumbled Ritz Crackers. Also, feel free to pop some Pork Belly Nuggets in your mouth. Glazed with a blueberry balsamic sauce, these sweet little piggies are de-lish!

Did my mentioning experimental cocktails prick up your ears? Then try the Tiger Tiger Woods, Y'all. Bourbon, cognac, black tea honey, lemon juice—it's the cocktail version of a hole-in-one. Then there's the

Donut Ice Cream Sandwich made with seasonal ice cream and a daily donut. Why do millennials get such a bad rap? Seems like they have all the good ideas these days!

MH ZH

$$

3536 Sunset Boulevard

SILVER LAKE

323-636-7598

Mh Zh is listed as an Israeli restaurant. The name derives from the Hebrew phrase, *mah zeh,* which basically translates as "What is this?"

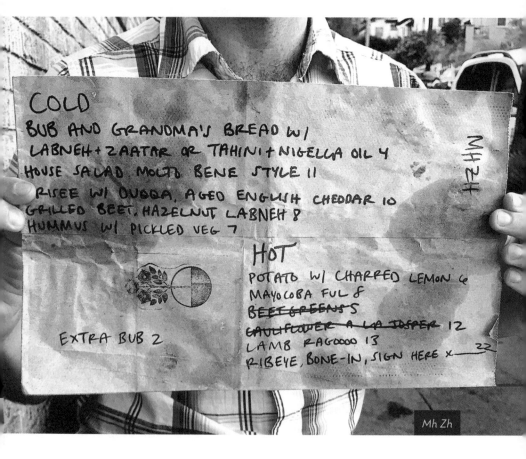

Mh Zh

Mh Zh

And that phrase may pop into your head more than a few times during your dining experience. First things first—there will be a line. You put your name on the list and you're told that there's limited seating, confined mostly to outside. You can try to squeeze into a small two-top inside with a full view of the open kitchen. Either way, you'll have to wait.

And when you do get that table, you're sitting on a milk crate, not a chair, and your dinner partner is sitting on a bucket. Then you notice that the menu is written out on large torn pieces of brown paper bag. Scribbled descriptions of the food makes it sort of hard to know what, exactly, you're ordering.

In situations like these, I find it best to just point at something.

Then (fingers crossed) hope it's delicious. Luckily, it always is. Last time, I started off with Tahini + Nigella Oil, served with rustic bread, as well as hummus and pickled vegetables. I also loved the Mayocoba Fun, a spicy bean puree with sumac and preserved lemon, and more bread. Main course all-star definitely has to be the Lamb Ragu, a bowl of flavorful, spicy lamb resting in a tahini puddle, garnished with fresh herbs.

The food here is intense and comforting at the same time. And it'll make you forget the fact that your butt is numb from sitting on a crate.

Pro tip: This place is BYOB.

BLUDSO'S BAR & QUE

$$

609 N La Brea Avenue

FAIRFAX

323-931-2583

barandque.com/bludsos

After serving for more than a decade in the Department of Corrections, BBQ maestro Kevin Bludso opened a namesake joint in the neighborhood that bore him: Compton. It quickly became a go-to destination for exquisitely smoked and seasoned ribs and brisket. Soon another spot opened on La Brea, solidifying Bludso's reputation as the King of Smoked Meats in LA. Bludso's style of BBQ is pure Texan (where the Bludso family roots were planted): big hunks of meat, cooked over a long period of time, served with sweetly tinged sauce. Not that the meat needs it. The spice-rubbed brisket is insanely tender. The ribs contain barely a trace of physical connection to the bone. There are hot links that snap like twigs with each bite. Get a side of stewed collard greens with chunks of ham hock mixed in, or the extra gooey macaroni and cheese. National Pie Champion Nicole Rucker heads up the dessert menu. Get a piece of the deeply rich Chocolate Chess Pie. Or else.

LALIBELA ETHIOPIAN RESTAURANT

$$

1025 S Fairfax Avenue

FAIRFAX

323-965-1025

lalibelala.com

Ethiopian restaurant Lalibela is a feast for all the senses. Most of the dishes come in eye-popping, kaleidoscopic colors; aromatic scents of spices and herbs; and, of course, palate-inspiring flavor. Your best bet is to bring friends, order a few plates, and share. For meat eaters, the Zilzil Tibs—strips of tender beef sautéed in spiced butter—is fantastic.

Ethiopian food is very vegetarian and vegan friendly. In fact, they have a dish called Veggie Utopia. This large, shareable plate is a combo of 14 different veggie dishes, which include a spiced lentil stew called Miser, cabbage, a spiced chickpea stew known as Shero, and green beans . . . just to name a few. Spread it out on top of injera—a spongy, sourdough Ethiopian flatbread. This is one of those meals where it's totally cool to eat with your hands—as long as it ends up in your mouth, of course.

Finally, for dessert, order up some ice cream with house-roasted Ethiopian coffee poured over it. You'll feel like you're in Addis Ababa.

BEAUTY & ESSEX

$$$

1615 Cahuenga Boulevard

HOLLYWOOD

323-676-8880

beautyandessex.com/los-angeles

Located in the heart of Tinseltown, not far from the corner of Hollywood and Vine, where lots of actors and actresses never get discovered, lies glitzy dining haven Beauty & Essex. With a menu conceived by restaurant impresario (and *Chopped* judge), Chris Santos,

B&E serves up a variety of small bites such as Red Snapper Tacos, Gem Salad with Champagne vinaigrette, and Grilled Cheese with Smoke Bacon and Tomato Soup Dumplings.

There's a raw bar to provide adequate aphrodisiacs, as well as an assortment of Jewels on Toast, including their Chicken Liver Mousse, made with a Rioja-braised shallot marmalade. Other Jewels to be mined are the Chicken Liver Mousse with shallot marmalade; Caesar Toast with creamy garlic and crisp chicken skin; and the Chicken Tinga Arepas (try saying that five times fast) with an utterly delectable cilantro-pistachio pesto and cotija cheese.

For the main course, there's Oven Braised Chicken Meatballs with sheep's milk ricotta; or try the Scallop & Pork Belly, their version of the classic surf 'n' turf. Beauty & Essex also has their own pawn shop on the premises, located in the front, where, if you so desire, you can buy a brand new Fender Guitar. I guess that's cool? Until you try splitting the check with a Telecaster, that is.

ROSE CAFE & RESTAURANT

$$

220 Rose Avenue

VENICE

310-399-0711

rosecafevenice.com

Around since 1979, Rose Cafe & Restaurant is one of the central eating spots in Venice Beach. Having recently completed a makeover, this place is good for anything from a drink at the bar to a night with friends out on the patio. And is that the entire first Strokes album playing over the speakers? Why, yes it is. Chef Jason Neroni is a big music fan and believes that a good rockin' vibe is almost as important as the food itself.

The menu at Rose Cafe centers around their fresh produce and unbelievable pasta dishes. There's also a raw bar and multiple meat and cheese plates, some of which hail all the way from France! And

Indiana—less classy, I know, but just as delicious. Whether it comes from a goat from Touraine, or a cow from French Lick, this place has some of the best, and most affordable, fromage around.

Did you come with a group? Then order for the table a plate of the Honey Lacquered Short Rib, served with a bone marrow chili jus. On a date? And does he or she have an impressive appetite? No judgments here. Then might I suggest the 28 Day Tomahawk Dry-Aged Ribeye. This hunk of meat is accompanied by grilled savoy cabbage, caramelized onions, and a smoked bacon marmalade.

But let's get back to those pastas, shall we? Can I entice you with a Smoked Radiatore Carbonara? What if I said it came with braised bacon and poached egg? Yeah, I thought you might be into that. Rose serves a Smoked Radiatore Carbonara with poached egg, braised bacon, and parmesan cheese. I'm no dietician, but I think that covers most of the major food groups.

The wine list includes many rosés and French or Italian reds. Got room for dessert? Perfect! You'll be having the Banana Pudding, a banana compote with candied hazelnuts, vanilla namelaka (basically an even creamier ganache), and whipped cream. Take that, diet!

SOTTO

$$$

9575 W Pico Boulevard

BEVERLY HILLS

310-277-0210

sottorestaurant.com

Looking for a charming, intimate setting, where the pizzas are top flight, the wine list is agonized over by somebody with a PhD till it's damn near perfect, and the pasta dishes are some of the best you'll ever devour? Then the southern Italy-inspired Sotto, Steve Samson's just-south-of-Beverly-Hills spot, is for you.

Ever wanted to have pork jowl as a pizza topping? Then order the

Guanciale pie, with ricotta and fennel pollen. There are large plates for sharing, such as the Brick-Pressed Half Chicken, with heirloom bean ragu, house-made pork sausage, and Tuscan kale. Or the Bistecca, a dry-aged ribeye served with arugula and fingerling potatoes. Bar Director Brynn Smith has reinvented the cocktail menu to include more rustic-centric spirits: the rye-based Rosa Bellini, with a squirt of lemon and a touch of sage, is quite refreshing. Cap it all off with a cappuccino paired with the Orange Creamiscle. Yes, it's as delicious as it sounds. This marvel of a dessert comes with panna cotta, toasted almonds, and hachiya persimmon cream. What a country we live in!

LUV2EAT THAI BISTRO

$$

6660 Sunset Boulevard

  HOLLYWOOD

323-498-5835

luv2eatthai.com

Hollywood's Luv2eat opened only a few years ago, but has already become one of LA's premiere Thai spots. Chefs Fern and Pla both hail from the province of Phuket, and you'll definitely be saying "Phuket" after looking over their menu—you know, cause you'll want one of everything. Anyway, the Jade Noodle with three BBQ meats is always a great choice. This beauty comes with BBQ pork, crispy pork, and roasted duck. The noodles have a very nice, and strong, kick of spice. It comes either dry or as a soup: go with the soup. One of my fave Thai dishes ever.

You'll also want to try the Phuket-style Crab Curry: vermicelli rice noodles with blue crab, served with hard-boiled egg, pickled carrot, and papaya. Just mix that baby all together and go to town. And what's that couple at the next table drinking? Sort of looks like Pepto Bismol? That, my friends, is called Pink Milk, a Thai standard. It's basically a sweeter strawberry milk but made with a syrup. It'll help ease the heat your taste buds have just been subjected to.

HERE'S LOOKING AT YOU

$$$

3901 W 6th Street

KOREATOWN

213-568-3573

hereslookingatyoula.com

Here's Looking at You is former Animal chef Jonathan Whitener's new zeitgeist restaurant, located in the middle of Koreatown. The flavors on this regularly rotating menu are bold and inventive: past favorites have included a beef tartare with red chiles, yolk, and pickled ramps; the spicy

Here's Looking at You

frog legs with salsa negra and lime; and veal sweetbreads with fennel, mustard, and sesame. Whitener is clearly swinging for the fences here. Each plate is a work of art. The pork belly is all fatty flavor and crisp texture—for sure a standout dinner option.

The cocktail menu is changed to include mostly seasonal ingredients, each paired with the musical artist that inspired its creation: the Figure Eight, for example, referencing LA icon Elliott Smith, is made with Singani 63, Lillet, Cocchi Americano, apricot, curaçao, bitter lemon soda, and seasonal fruit. A perfect LA drink. For dessert, get the Yuzu Tart, an Asian version of lemon meringue. HLAY is one of the most exciting restaurants in the city. You can tell

Here's Looking at You

because I didn't even use exclamation points to hype my description. This place don't need no stinking exclamation points. HLAY *is* an exclamation point.

SALAZAR

$$

2490 N Fletcher Drive

FROGTOWN

salazarla.com

Quickly becoming one of the city's go-to destinations for mingling under the stars, Salazar features a gorgeous outdoor patio, not far from the LA River, to enjoy some fancy-ass tacos and a cool breeze/ drink. Located in the formerly gang-infested neighborhood known as Frogtown, Salazar gives off an Arizonian vibe: desert landscaping, cacti, and the smell of mesquite coming from the smoker.

The tacos are the thing here. Drool-worthy Al Pastor with cilantro, red onion, and pineapple; big, juicy chunks of Pollo Asado; and the Vegetable taco with grilled cauliflower, carrots, roasted fennel, and pickled ramps. If tacos won't satisfy your hunger, they do a perfect Hanger Steak as well. The bar serves a variety of cocktails from Margaritas (naturally) to micheladas. Salazar is the perfect place to meet up with the gang. Uh, not that gang. That would be bad.

CHI SPACCA

$$$$

6610 Melrose Avenue

HANCOCK PARK

323-297-1133

chispacca.com

This ain't your dad's steakhouse. Nope. From Mozza's Nancy Silverton comes this neo-carnivore spot that *Food & Wine* magazine described as a "Meat Speakeasy"—but let's hope the vice squad isn't busting in anytime soon. Chi Spacca is quaint, with a view of the open kitchen, the complete antithesis of what you might picture as a steakhouse—no lacquered wood walls, no waiter in his 60s with bushy eyebrows. Their first claim to fame was installing the first "dry cure" program in LA. Basically, they get pretty wild with their charcuterie plates, which they call Salumeria. Try the Whole Muscles plate with ciccioli and capocollo. On the main entree side, or Macelleria, how could you not go with the Beef & Bone Marrow Pie? Perfectly salted beef cheek with funghi encased in a pie crust. With mint yogurt and cilantro, the "Moorish" Lamb Shoulder Chop is another standout.

Your knowledgeable waiter will help you pair a bold wine with your meat. Lastly, get your Instagram ready—for dessert it's the Butterscotch Budino: a rich pudding with sea salt and rosemary pine nut cookies.

BAROO

$$

5706 Santa Monica Boulevard

EAST HOLLYWOOD

323-645-7041

baroola.strikingly.com

Owner-chef Kwang Uh is blazing a new path in Korean fusion. Interested in combining natural ingredients with fermentation techniques, Uh's East Hollywood location has already been a semifinalist in the James Beard Awards. Baroo is a test kitchen, which means that things don't usually stay on the menu for long.

Some past menu items of note have been Shrimp Toast, Kimchi Fried Rice with pineapple-fermented kimchi and quinoa, and the Noorook. This beautiful plate is made of mixed grains such as Job's tears, kamut, and farro, roasted koi beet cream, toasted seeds, and macadamia nuts. Colorful, creamy, and with a bit of tanginess, it's a real treat. Or how can you pass on something called Asian Fever? The bowl includes Amira basmati rice (deep fried!), crispy shrimp, and lime supreme, which is basically a wedge of lime minus the skin, pith, membranes, and seeds. Otherwise known as the useless parts. I got the fever all right, and the only cure is another serving of that!

Speaking of fermentation—definitely start the whole meal off with a Pickle Sampler. A wide range of veggies, fermented for who knows how long, but loaded with flavor. Be prepared to wait for a table—this place is small and fills up fast.

5

FOREVER SINCE BREAKFAST (LATE NIGHT)

"I went to a restaurant that serves 'breakfast at any time.'
So I ordered French Toast during the Renaissance."

—Steven Wright

One of my favorite paintings is "Nighthawks" by Edward
Hopper. I saw it as a young boy at the Art Institute of
Chicago on a trip to visit my older sister, who at the
time was living in the Windy City. The painting depicts a
New York City diner at night. There are three customers:
a couple sitting close together, who seem to be either
estranged lovers or strangers falling in love. Another man
sits left of frame, his back to us. A blond boy in white (coat,
cap) inside the counter, mid-chore. Nobody is eating—there

are no plates in front of them. Just coffee mugs. The man with his back toward us has a saltshaker handy, perhaps used to cut the acidity of his cup of joe? Nor does a conversation between any of the characters seem to be occurring. Everyone is lost in their own world, the world they are sharing with the other occupants. They are alone, together.

I myself spent many years as a nighthawk. From my time living in New Orleans, where certain bars and clubs never close, to finally settling in Los Angeles, a nightscape that inspired everyone from Raymond Chandler and Tom Waits—who also loved Hopper's painting—to Ridley Scott and the great Arthur Lee.

My mother once said, "Nothing good happens after midnight," which is her version of "The freaks come out at night." She feared that troubling influences would eventually find their way to me. Boy, did she hit the nail on head!

As I get older and wiser, my sleep patterns have made a complete reversal. Now I'm an early riser, having gone to bed at a decent hour. My mother appreciates it.

Despite its undeserved rap as a city that shuts down early—which may well be changing in a big way if a newly proposed 4 a.m. bar curfew takes effect—Los Angeles has its fair share of late-evening diners and hangs, places where you can get a decent slice of pizza, pie, or life. You can have a Fruity Pebble-crusted donut, a bacon-wrapped hot dog, a stack of pancakes that touches the ceiling, or a plate of steaming hot dumplings late into the night.

So spend the day running errands or grinding it out at the old 9 to 5. Meet some friends for drinks, have a few laughs, eat a full and satisfying meal. Sooner or later, your crew will stagger off, complaining that they have to get up early. But you still have the itch—you want to stay out. You want to get up to no good. I get it. I've been there. I am no longer there, but I can describe *there* in great detail. And now you can benefit from the fruits of my misspent youth. Enjoy! Just don't let my mother catch you out so late.

BIRDIES

$$ (unless you get the gold donut—then it's $$$$)

314 W Olympic Boulevard

`DTLA`

213-536-5270

birdiesla.com

Birdies in DTLA opens every Friday morning at 7 a.m. and then doesn't close their doors till 8 p.m. on *Sunday*. That's like . . . I don't know, I'm bad at math, but it's a lot of consecutive hours being open.

So if you find yourself out on a Saturday at 3 a.m. with an unbeliev-able hankering for a Candied Bacon Maple donut, one that goes well with a breast and wing of fried chicken and a hot cup of coffee, get yourself to Birdies, stat! That should satisfy you (and keep you awake) till Sunday around 7 p.m.—at which point you have to do it all over again.

Birdies

It's like being stuck in a Steely Dan song, but without the red velvet backing vocals of Michael McDonald.

But if you're like me, then you're insanely rich and LOVE to flaunt it. And when I'm at Birdies I impress everybody in the place by throwing down a crispy Benjamin Franklin and having me a bite of their Solid Gold donut. You read that correctly: Solid Gold. Or for 100 bucks you could get about three dozen of the Lemon Thyme Pistachio, which is also dynamite. It's your savings account.

CANTER'S DELI

$$

419 N Fairfax Avenue

FAIRFAX

323-651-2030

cantersdeli.com

If this place is good enough for Slash from Guns N' Roses to hang out at, then by gum, it's good enough for you mere mortals. Canter's has been in the pastrami and corned beef slinging business for nearly 90 years. In Los Angeles, that practically qualifies it as a Roman ruin.

Canters

Speaking of pastrami, there's always been an unofficial contest of sorts for best pastrami sandwich in LA (we've said our piece, elsewhere), and while the hot pastrami sammie at this Fairfax joint might not come out on top, it's still quite good. I've had many a quality late-night meal here with friends, munching on latkes (potato pancakes) and onion rings, washing it all down with an orange cream milkshake.

Another big plus—the bar attached to the side of Canter's, The Kibbitz Room, has hosted some of the best rock bands in the city, and sometimes still does.

BEST ICE CREAM

Once you're done wining and dining your date, or attorney, nothing is a better post-dinner treat than a scoop (or three) of ice cream! These are the spots I scream about when asked about ice cream. I'll stop screaming now.

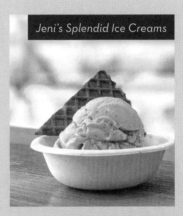

Jeni's Splendid Ice Creams

10. Jeni's Splendid Ice Creams (Los Feliz)

9. Magpies Softserve (Silver Lake)

8. McConnell's Fine Ice Creams (Studio City)

7. Milk (West Hollywood)

6. Wanderlust Creamery (Atwater)

5. Carmela (Pasadena)

4. Scoops (Hollywood)

3. Salt & Straw (West Hollywood)

2. Mashti Malone's Ice Cream (Hollywood)

1. Sweet Rose Creamery (Fairfax)

Salt & Straw

CARNEY'S

$

8351 Sunset Boulevard

323-654-8300

carneytrain.com

Carney's was where I had my first true celebrity sighting. I had moved to LA about a week prior, and often found myself wandering the Sunset Strip, after bombing at the Comedy Store. Despite bombing, I still love stand-up comedy. I also love hot dogs. And Carney's is open till 3 a.m.

So there I was enjoying one of their namesake dogs (chili, mustard, tomato, and onions) when I looked up and spotted a certain all denim-wearing, car-loving, now-retired talk show host (rhymes with Day Steno). He ordered two Red Barons (spicy Polish dog, red cabbage, mustard, Cheddar cheese) and sat down right next to me. With double napkins so as not to get mustard on his sky-blue shirt, he chowed down. I must've been staring for an obnoxious amount of time, because he gave me a look and said, "What? You've never seen an Italian eat before?" I smiled and went back to my own food.

Weirdly enough, it was just enough of an interaction to give me the confidence to continue hitting the clubs and telling my jokes, whether the audiences laughed or not. I'm not exactly Dane Cook, yet, but I've got a tight five minutes ready to go if Day Steno ever decides to go back in the talk show business. Or I could just wait around this trolley-car restaurant for him to reappear and perform directly to him.

BOB'S BIG BOY

$$

4211 W Riverside Drive

BURBANK

818-843-9334

bobs.net

I'm no food snob, as I think I've demonstrated by now. But Bob's Big Boy might in some people's estimation be a step too far in the anti-snob direction. Those people would be wrong. Periodically, I like to check and make sure Bob's Big Boy in Burbank (say that five times fast) still delivers on the double beef patty side of things. Fret not, friends, the "Super" Big Boy Combo is still bigger than your head, and twice as delicious! They also have salads, but nobody's perfect. After your meal, make sure to take a selfie with the Big Boy statue out front. It was featured in *Austin Powers*, remember? That's probably as close to a celebrity sighting as you're gonna get in this neck of the woods.

THE CORNER DOOR

$$

12477 W Washington Boulevard

CULVER CITY

310-313-5810

thecornerdoorla.com

Serving late-night bites till 1 a.m., Culver City's the Corner Door is a must-do late-evening hang. And who doesn't love a place that offers Fish and Chips past midnight? Nobody who would bother picking up this book, that's who. One of my best friends swears by their Moscow Mule. In lieu of booze, I go with the Sticky Toffee Pudding. And yet somehow I still end up drunk-dialing my ex.

CHATEAU MARMONT

$$$

8221 Sunset Boulevard

WEST HOLLYWOOD

323-656-1010

chateaumarmont.com

You could say that the Chateau on the Sunset Strip has a colorful history. It's been a haven for celebrities and wannabes for decades now. Some come here to party, some come to trash hotel rooms, and some to breathe their last breaths. And so it goes. Every day, a new batch of guests arrive to push the limits of mortality. But first, a killer hamburger at 4 a.m.! Partying with Lindsay Lohan really works up an appetite. J/K. Well, not really, but for legal reasons I have to say that.

But I'm not joshing about that burger—it's simple AF: lettuce, tomato, onion, house pickles, with a slice of melted Cheddar, but it's so damn good. I also enjoy munching on Black Truffle Arancini—a most delectable 'shroom.

IZZY'S DELI

$$

1433 Wilshire Boulevard

SANTA MONICA

310-394-1131

izzysdeli.com

LA is defiantly—proudly, even—the "city that *does* sleep." Unlike the Big Apple, or the Big Easy, or even the Big Chicago, there are very few all-night, never-closed, come-whenever-the-hell-you-like restaurants. Even fewer on the West Side. Izzy's in Santa Monica is a rare exception. Open since 1973, Izzy's is a traditional New York deli that happens to be near the Pacific Ocean—which could explain why the Crab Cake Sliders are so damn tasty. You're not gonna find those in Greenpoint after last call.

Izzy's also has primo chili that can either be served in a bowl or slathered on a burger, a hot dog, or fries. How's that for democracy?

TACO ZONE

$

1342 N Alvarado Street

ECHO PARK

Best. Taco. Truck. In. LA. You may have noticed (or not) that, thus far, I have refrained from labeling any such place as the best of its kind. Except for Langer's—but that was solely about a particular sandwich. Not the whole restaurant. You'll also observe that Taco Zone is not mentioned in the food truck chapter. Truth be told, Taco Zone deserves an entire book of its own, such is its excellence. I have many fond memories of hitting this truck after a fantastic night in the City of Angels.

Taco Zone

What should you order here? Good question. From the al pastor to the veggie option, Taco Zone tacos are legit in their own way, but what they do better than anyone, or at least anyone on four wheels, is suadero. It's a thin cut of beef from between the belly and the leg on the cow. It usually has a super smooth texture—no muscle grain. Fry it up and it's the perfect taco filling. I always ask the servers to fry it a bit longer than usual, which adds some smokiness.

Taco Zone is also well known for their variety of sauces, each in their own two-gallon bucket, in a series of colors that range from Kermit green (salsa verde) to Blood Red Lava Lamp (super-hot chili sauce). Choose your sauce, sprinkle on some diced onions and cilantro, take a bite of your taco of choice, and you'll see why I raved about this place. As with many of the recommendations in this book, there will be a line,

Taco Zone

pretty much from open to close. The upside to living in a place that's in the middle of a historic drought is that it almost never rains. So lines, while inconvenient, are rarely misery-inducing.

JOHNNIE'S PASTRAMI

$$

4017 Sepulveda Boulevard

CULVER CITY

310-397-6654

johnniespastrami.com

Serving up paper-thin, lean-cut pastrami sandwiches since your parents met, Culver City's own Johnnie's Pastrami is a perfect end to any night. Or every night. Boy, you must really like pastrami.

You'll feel like you either went back to the future or somehow ended up in the movie *Back to the Future* (either is possible) with tiny but loud jukeboxes at every booth. You'll wanna dance all night. This place is so drenched in the '50s, they're still cash only. Make sure you get a side of onion rings, which feature holes so wide you can drive a Studebaker through them.

TOMMY'S ORIGINAL WORLD FAMOUS HAMBURGERS

$

2575 Beverly Boulevard

WESTLAKE

213-389-9060

originaltommys.com

There are quite a few Original Tommy's Hamburgers scattered throughout the city, but this Original is the original Original, started as a ramshackle stand on the corner of Beverly and Rampart in 1946. So clearly they know what they're doing here at Tommy's—and what they do is smother their burgers in chili. That chili-smothering empire has expanded beyond just LA. You'll find locations in San Diego, Orange, Ventura, and somewhere in Nevada.

LUCKY BOY DRIVE-IN

$

640 S Arroyo Parkway

PASADENA

626-793-0120

luckyboyburgers.com

Nothing like receiving your meal in a box and bag. That's what you get when your name is called at Lucky Boy in Pasadena. Whatever it is that you ordered—be it burger, burrito, hot dog—every item comes packed the same way: waxy bag inside a cardboard box. You'll see rows of people at the patio tables, all grubbing from a box. It would be mildly off-putting if the food weren't so good.

The burgers here are pretty basic, which is fine by me. Lucky Boy is the go-to place for little old ladies (and everybody else) from Pasadena. There was even a popular Facebook page dedicated to one of their cashiers: some guy named Ted who had an affinity for shouting out orders and keeping the line moving. In fact, Ted was downright rude. And yet people still came in droves, so what does that tell you about the food here? Or possibly about some people's self-esteem?

THE MISFIT

$$

225 Santa Monica Boulevard

SANTA MONICA

310-656-9800

themisfitbar.com

The Misfit prides itself on being Santa Monica's cocktail bar. It's got a retro cool decor (their sign is hard to miss) and enough comfort food

on the menu to get you through the night. They serve the entire menu late into the evening, which means you can get their Misfit Burger right before last call. Grass-fed beef, Cheddar, all the fixings, with mayo and house-made pickles. Be brave and throw a cage-free egg on top. Or be even braver and order the Crispy Chicken sandwich, which the bartender warns is f&$&ing spicy.

The Misfit also serves small-batch gelato from Grateful Spoon—pistachio for me, please!

PACIFIC DINING CAR

$$$$

1310 W 6th Street

DTLA

213-483-6000

pacificdiningcar.com

Located next to the Good Samaritan Hospital in DTLA, Pacific Dining Car has been serving up only the highest-quality Prime American beef for "God only knows" how long (obligatory Beach Boys reference). They age their own steaks, which greatly enhances the flavor and tenderness of the beef. Once cut up by the butcher, the steaks are then treated to an open flame, courtesy of their uniquely designed grill, which allows the juices and flavor of the beef to come to the fore. And it's not just the steaks that receive precise attention—the entire restaurant (yes, it is an actual dining car) is spotless. The wood-paneled walls are expertly preserved. The tablecloths are immaculate.

The late-night menu offers a diverse selection of dishes, from French Toast to a Reuben Sandwich, and Maine Lobster Truffled Mac & Cheese. You can still get an eight-ounce Filet Mignon at any hour. It's $40, but you're worth it.

The vibe at Santa Monica's retro diner, Swingers, is best described as '60s chic: all peace signs, American flags, and a Jane Fonda arrest photo. There are a good deal of vegetarian and vegan options on the menu, including avocado toast topped with olive oil, salt, lemon, and chili flakes. I recommend the Vegan Burrito with sautéed tofu and spinach, quinoa, and black beans, all wrapped up in a whole-wheat tortilla.

I once saw Beck sitting in a booth here, sometime in the George W. Bush years. He had in front of him a plate of avocados, all of which were perfectly ripe, cut into long pieces. That's it. I watched as he ate each one

Swingers

separately. Think of all the great menu items he could've ordered, and he went with just that. What a loser, baby.

IL TRAMEZZINO

$$

454 N Canon Drive

BEVERLY HILLS

310-273-0501

iltram.net

When you think of Beverly Hills, it's probably images of a Kardashian or Hilton flashing some major bling while being followed by swarms of paparazzi. What you probably DON'T think about is you enjoying an incredible Black Forest Ham panini at 3 a.m., after a long day of snapping photos of undeserving celebrities. But that's exactly what Il Tramezzino is all about. This is a place to see and be seen. Or be seen seeing. They also serve a variety of Tramezzinis—or Italian finger sandwiches. No, there's not actually fingers in the . . . never mind. I could probably eat 20 of their Caprese tramezzinis. Could? I mean, have.

Make sure to check out the dessert menu, which features a lot of yumminess imported directly from Milan. Can't go wrong with a Classic Cannoli. Unless you try to eat two at once and end up with an embarrassing picture in *US Weekly*. But, hey, there's no such thing as bad publicity.

BCD TOFU HOUSE

$$

3575 Wilshire Boulevard

KOREATOWN

213-382-6677

bcdtofu.com

Nicknamed "The House that Tofu Built," this mini chain has been serving up that delicious little spongy fare since 1996. BCD is named after the Korean city Bukchang Dong.

The Wilshire location is open all hours of the day, serves alcohol, and is probably gonna be your new favorite place to order Spicy Raw Crab. But don't be a fool and pass on the dumplings—that's their specialty.

LOS TACOS

$

7954 Santa Monica Boulevard

WEST HOLLYWOOD

323-848-9141

Doesn't look like much from the outside, but Los Tacos, located in a WeHo strip mall, fully delivers on your burrito dreams. Go with either the beef or chicken—I like both. At the same time. And you can get chips and salsa for just a buck.

HODORI

$

1001 S Vermont Avenue

PICO-UNION

213-383-3554

myhodori.com

For those of you craving Korean comfort food in the wee hours of the night, classic joint Hodori will do you right. Where do we begin? Well, for starters, there are numerous stews that are simply delectable; most notably, the boiled ox feet stew with rice, or "Woo Jok Tang" for the native speaker. I'm also high on the Galbi Tang—that's short rib soup with rice.

On the noodle side of the menu, go with the Dak Gae Jang, which is a hot spicy chicken with, you guessed it, rice.

FRED 62

$$

1850 N Vermont Avenue

LOS FELIZ

323-667-0062

fred62.com

Having just celebrated their 20th anniversary, Fred 62 is still a stomping ground for the young and diverse Los Feliz crowd. Since bringing back

co-founder and original chef, Fred Eric, they've revamped the menu, focusing on higher-end diner cuisine. But this is still a place where you can grab a quality burger (dubbed the Juicy Lucy) or a plate of Mac n' Cheese Balls.

The Late Night menu includes Waffle Sliders (fried chicken served on a mini waffle with kale spiced maple aioli and mustard greens) and Frito Pies. What is the Frito Pie, you ask? It's a bag of Fritos with brisket chili poured inside, topped with jack and Cheddar cheese and roasted poblano sour cream. It's actually quite tasty. For those searching for a unique dessert selection, Fred's got you covered. Besides mastering milkshakes and Dark Chocolate Malt Brownies, they bake what they have named Punk Tarts, which are basically house-made Pop-Tarts.

QUE RICOS

$

12940 Victory Boulevard

NORTH HOLLYWOOD

818-985-8014

quericosmexicankitchen.com

This little neon-lit shack located in North Hollywood is known to get quite busy late at night. Full of patrons fresh from work or the bar, Que Ricos offers a variety of proteins usually reserved for adventurous food trucks and not fast food spots.

Here, you can get Lengua, Buche, and Cabeza. Or, as your anatomy book calls them, Tongue, Belly, and Head. Yum! Get your burrito wet or dry (I always opt for wet) and load it up with sauces. For special occasions, try the Super Nachos, which, at their low, low price, is the best bang for your nacho around.

TENTENYU

$$

3849 Main Street

CULVER CITY

420-603-4803

tentenyu-us.com

Tentenyu are masters of chicken ramen. The broth is simmered with bones and feet (and a bit of pork), which always comes out rich, creamy, and damn delicious. I'm here for the signature namesake ramen: three sliced chashu, menma, green onions, and bean sprouts. I usually add black garlic oil for that little extra kick. The Pork Fried Rice is another can't-miss dish.

MAO'S KITCHEN

$$

1512 Pacific Avenue

VENICE

310-581-8305

maoskitchen.com

Communism looks good on paper. In practice, it's a disaster. The menu at Mao's Kitchen, named after the once-venerated Red China leader, also looks good on paper. But it is the opposite of disaster—it's like the unfettered free market of Chinese grub!

If you've spent the night in Venice wading in the Pacific Ocean, dodging tiger sharks and dreadlocked surfers, make your way to Mao's for their Kungpao Chicken, loaded with onions, green onions, bell peppers, carrots, peanuts, and Sichuan pepper. It packs quite a punch. For dessert, they have Chocolate Pineapple, which is a giant slice of pineapple served with a warm chocolate dipping sauce. Once you try it, you won't want to eat pineapple any other way. But you'll probably have to, at some point. Sorry.

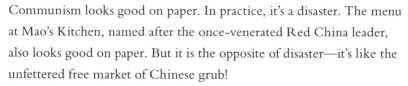

LA CABAÑA

$$

738 Rose Avenue

VENICE

310-392-7973

lacabanavenice.com

Serving fine, family-style Mexican food in Venice Beach for more than 50 years, La Cabaña stays open every night till 3 a.m., or as I call it, Nachos Grande time! This is one stacked plate of tortilla chips, cheese, beans, and guacamole. La Cabaña has their own wood-fired stove where they make all of the chips and tortillas. The Cheese Enchiladas are better than decent too.

AGRA CAFE

$$

4325 Sunset Boulevard

SILVER LAKE

323-665-7890

agracafeonline.com

LA is home to more than its fair share of good Indian restaurants, but my personal favorite is Silver Lake's Agra. Everything is awesome, from their yellow Lentil (Dal) Soup, slowly simmered in broth, to their signature Balti dishes (basically a rich and hearty stew that is a nice balance of hot and sweet). Served with sides of rice and garnished with yogurt and fresh tomatoes, stews of lamb, chicken, shrimp, or fish are Agra specialties. Make sure to get an order of Garlic Naan to help soak up all this goodness. Finally, Agra serves for dessert a sublime Pistachio Ice Cream that buys them a small piece of my heart forever.

WURSTKÜCHE

$$

800 E 3rd Street

ARTS DISTRICT

213-687-4444

wurstkuche.com

Advertising that you serve exotic sausages till 1:30 in the morning could raise the eye of vice officers everywhere, but either Wurstküche is paid-up on their cop bribes, or even law enforcement can't resist these big, plump, juicy wieners. The menu is divided into three categories: Classics, Gourmet, and Exotic. On the Classic side, I like the Bockwurst (veal, pork, and spices). For Gourmet, go with the Austin Blues (hot and spicy smoked pork). On the Exotic end of things, you would be a fool and forever regretful if you didn't go with the Pheasant with Herbs de Provence. Get yourself a side of thick-cut Belgian Fries and a beer as big as a Buick.

6

HOORAY FOR FOOD TRUCKS

"The taco honors the truck."

—Jonathan Gold

Everybody in LA has *their* truck. The truck they brag to their friends about discovering, like a speakeasy. They know where and at what time to be there to eat the best tacos, or fried chicken sandwich, even deep-fried Oreos. Well, guess what? I know ALL the trucks. And now I'm gonna pass along my knowledge to you, dear readers.

But, first, a little history.

The year 2008 saw a new version of the Wild West in Los Angeles. Mobile kitchens, aided by a new app called Twitter, were setting up shop all around the city. And one of the first stars of the food truck scene was chef Roy Choi with his Korean-fusion truck, Kogi. Foodies were tweeting endlessly about Choi's signature Short Rib Tacos. After a million or so FAVs & RTs, other chefs and restaurateurs caught on, purchased themselves a truck, and so began the food truck craze.

Also playing a role was the financial crisis of that era. Rents for restaurant space were astronomical; some chefs twigged to the incredibly low overhead a truck can offer (most trucks have only one or two cooks working at a time, as opposed to a fully staffed kitchen). Not that the only requirements for starting a food truck were as simple as kicking the tires and lighting the fires. You needed the right kind of crew, one that could work fast in cramped spaces. Many of them had to pull double duty as cook and cashier. There was no distinction between front or back of the house—everybody was front and center.

The city quickly realized the potential on their end to make money from these modern-day chuck wagons. For the food truck owners, suddenly there were new permits and licenses to acquire, not to mention parking restrictions to deal with. Other cities, such as New York, have a limit on the amount of truck permits that they will issue, but Los Angeles eventually was smart enough to realize that their streets were more than capable of handling dozens and dozens of trucks on a daily basis. To this day, you can see an entire block lined with trucks. As well as swarms of hungry people.

Of course, the food had to be good, or this was all just a novelty. Luckily for us foodies, chefs treated their trucks with as much respect and attention to detail (and taste) as they afforded their brick-and-mortar establishments. Soon enough, there were trucks for any type of craving you may have: tacos, grilled cheese, seafood, even straight-up carnival grub. All you had to do was check Twitter to see where these trucks would be parked and get in line. And while Twitter helped trucks establish themselves, Instagram only pushed the hype further. As they say, a picture is worth a thousand words.

But were food trucks restaurants? Even though truckloads (sorry) of cash were being made, the mobile food industry still seemed to lack a certain legitimacy. That all changed in 2014 when chef Wes Avila's truck, Guerrilla Tacos, landed at #13 on *LA Times* food critic Jonathan Gold's "101 Best Restaurants" list. It was the gold star that the food truck scene had been waiting for.

So what lies ahead for the food truckers? Or for their devoted customers? Self-driving trucks? How about food drones? My apartment complex has roof access—somebody drop off some tacos, stat!

In the meantime, here's a list of my favorite rolling restaurants.

 ## THE LOBOS TRUCK

thelobostruck.com

Twitter @TheLobosTruck

The Lobos Truck pride themselves on making "kick ass comfort food," the kind of food that makes you nostalgic for the days when gaining weight was something only old squares had to worry about. Now I'm one of those old squares. And yet I can't resist the taste of Lobos' Wachos. What in tarnation are Wachos? Crisscross-cut fries smothered in nacho toppings. The OG Wachos come with everything. And I do mean everything. Especially cheese. Wanna press your luck? Or meet your maker? Then go with the Heart Attack Wachos with roasted pork belly, jalapeño ranch dressing, and a sauce so hot they named it after the devil him(or her)self, Diablo. Yeah, it's pretty hot.

Off the grill, there's The Big Lobo: ⅓-pound grass-fed burger with jalapeño ranch, Cheddar, bacon, and a fried egg on a perfectly buttery brioche bun. For you non-animal eaters, there's The Portlander: a veggie patty, caramelized onion, Cheddar, vegan garlic aioli, and tomato.

FREE RANGE

freerangela.com

Instagram @freerangela

Free Range's fried-chicken breakfast sandwiches are out of this world—except, lucky you, they're not really out of this world. They're right here in LA, which some people think is a world of its own—but that's their problem. You should definitely get the Famous Avocado Toast: thick-cut sourdough bread from the Clark Street Bakery with an over-easy egg cooked inside, smashed avocado, pickled onions, and a drizzle of Sriracha. And they aren't above adding a bunch of bacon pieces to it, either. Wash it all down with an ice-cold ginger beer.

PICO HOUSE

picohouse.com

Instagram @picohouse

Pico House is a little confusing for two reasons: for starters, it's not a house. It's a food truck. Secondly, I've only once or twice seen it parked on Pico Boulevard. Other than that, this place is aces!

The truck was started by three lifelong friends who brought along a few other people to craft their now-famous grain bowls. This is the healthy side of the food truck world. Basically, each bowl is packed with grains, veggies, and your choice of protein. All are delicious and none will leave you with that "ugh, I overdid it" feeling. The grain mix includes barley, farro, red winter, rye, white wheat, and glenn wheat berry. Full of fiber, full of flavor.

My bowl of choice is the Union Lamb. The lamb is sautéed with onions and peppers, with a minty tomato and cucumber salad on top. For texture, there's a carrot puree that the lamb nestles on. As a Greek person, I'll overlook the use of goat cheese instead of feta. But only because it's still delicious. Get a refreshing Ugly Fruit Drank, their homemade punch made with imperfect fruits found at farmers' markets.

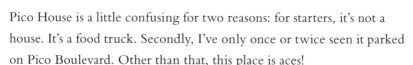

PRINCE OF VENICE

princeofvenicefoodtruck.com

Instagram @princeofvenicefoodtruck

When you think *food truck*, visions of staple food items probably pop into your brainpan: tacos, fried chicken sandwiches, maybe some sushi—but what if I told you there's a truck driving around that produces pasta dishes that rival anything you would find in Italy? Prince of Venice is that truck, *paisan*.

Prince of Venice is the brainchild of Emanuele Filiberto, the grandson of the last reigning king of Italy, and acclaimed Milan-born chef Mirko Paderno. Both had a desire to serve fresh pasta made with only the highest-quality ingredients. That's why the menu is constantly changing. The last time I was there, they had Macceroni alla Bolognese. This dish features ground beef and Bolognese sauce with sprinkles of Parmesan. I couldn't believe it: a truly classic, and delicious, Italian meal from a four-wheeler. And apparently, the plan is to add more trucks! Buon viaggio!

 ## THE GRILLED CHEESE TRUCK

thegrilledcheesetruck.com

Instagram @grilledcheesetruckla

My Achilles' heel is the grilled cheese sandwich. To me, there is no more comforting food than gooey, melted cheese between two slices of buttered and grilled bread. The simplicity of the dish is what really makes it. Grilled cheese is for kings and paupers. Anyone can make it, but only a select few make it an art.

And the Grilled Cheese Truck is an Old Master. The Plain & Simple Melt is, well, plain and simple. For more adventurous types, The Cheesy Mac 'n' Rib with smoked BBQ pork, southern macaroni, and caramelized onions might suffice. Or if you really went to go all out, have your dinner and dessert all in one bite. Behold! The S'mores Melt. Toasted marshmallows, Nutella, and crumbled graham crackers on brioche bread.

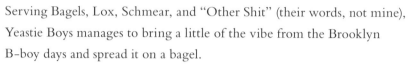

YEASTIE BOYS

yeastieboysbagels.com

Instagram @yeastieboysbagels

Serving Bagels, Lox, Schmear, and "Other Shit" (their words, not mine), Yeastie Boys manages to bring a little of the vibe from the Brooklyn B-boy days and spread it on a bagel.

Usually posting up in front of any one of four excellent coffee shops, my bagel of choice is the Game Over: soft scrambled egg, peppered bacon, sliced tomato, beer cheese (!), and jalapeño spread on a Cheddar bagel. Add a little avocado, cold brew from whatever destination they arrived at, and we are golden, my friend. Not literally. It's an expression.

EL FLAMIN' TACO

elflamintaco.com

@ElFlaminTaco

It's not hard to spot one of the many El Flamin' Taco trucks that park around the city at night: bright red and yellow paint job, LED lights

El Flamin' Taco

circling the top, lines around the block. El Flamin' Taco are as good as the principles they support. On their truck are numerous stickers and signs for causes as diverse as gay rights, AIDS awareness, and, of course, legal weed.

But back to the grub. On the menu at El Flamin' Taco is a scrumptious California Burrito, filled with pastrami, Cheddar, avocado, sour cream, and fries.

Most items on the menu here are dynamite, though, including the pastor straight off the pit. Put on your best virtue-signaling attire and head toward the rosy glow of El Flamin' Taco!

For reasons unbeknownst to anyone except (presumably) themselves, Tacos Quetzalcoatl is only open four days out of the week, closes shop mid-afternoon, and can't be found on weekends.

TQ serves made-to-order tortillas with some damn good salsas and distinctive meats such as chicharron and chorizo. The lamb is especially tasty, as well as the barbacoa that's served with a bone.

KOGI BBQ

kogibbq.com

Instagram @kogibbq

Chef Roy Choi's Korean BBQ truck remains the Acme of Los Angeles food trucks, logging miles and slinging BBQ since 2008. Try their signature dish: Kogi Kimchi Quesadilla. For the uninitiated, kimchi is a staple in Korean cuisine, made from fermented and salted vegetables, such as cabbage and Korean radishes. It's apparently very healthy for you, despite which I love it.

The quesadilla is mouthwatering, but you won't go wrong with the Short Rib Tacos either. Or the Spicy Pork Tacos! Damn, those are out of sight too. There's a reason why this truck has been top of the class for nearly a decade.

COOLHAUS

eatcoolhaus.com

Instagram @coolhaus

Cofounders Natasha Case and Freya Estreller were already baking cookies on the reg when they got the Nobel-worthy idea of combining their cookies with tempting ice cream flavors. After taking the 2009 Coachella festival by storm, Coolhaus was born.

My favorite sammie is mos def the Dirty Mint Chip between Snickerdoodle cookies. But there are so many unbelievable ice cream

flavors here to choose from. Let me name but a few: Brown Butter Candied Bacon, Avocado Sea Salt, Foie Gras PB & J, Fried Chicken and Waffles (yes, you read that right), and Pistachio Black Truffle.

And on the cookie side of things: Coffee Cake Whoopie Pie, S'mores, Vegan Ginger Molasses, and Pumpkin Pecan.

I wonder at which flavor you stopped reading and ran out to find this truck? I'm already in line.

PLANT FOOD FOR PEOPLE

pffp.org

Instagram @plantfoodforppl

Most food trucks are what you might call meat-centric. The pickings for our vegetarian brothers and sisters are, at best, slim. Not the case at Plant Food for People.

This truck offers a wide range of delectable meals from vegetable-based ingredients. But don't think the food here isn't venturesome. In fact, you've never really ventured till you try their #4 Jackfruit Taco. Stuffed with jackfruit, pinto beans, chipotle mayo, tomatillo salsa, coleslaw, and pico de gallo, it'll blow your argyle socks off. If you catch them on a Tuesday morning, make sure to order specific-to-that-day-only breakfast tacos made with potato and tofu. Mark this one a win for Veggie Nation!

LET'S BE FRANK

letsbefrankdogs.com

Twitter @LetsBeFrank

Let me be frank: The Let's Be Frank truck serves the best cased meats on four wheels in the city. Their hot dogs are grass-fed, so if, like me, you're imagining a hot dog grazing out in an open field, you would be correct. Free of hormones, antibiotics, nitrates, and everything else the FDA says "sure, why not?" to, you can enjoy these wieners relatively guilt-free.

The signature Frank Dog is a classic, bare-bones California grass-fed delight. Squeeze a little mustard and relish on there and you've got something special on your bun. If organic, pasture-raised meat isn't your thing, then there's the "Not" Dog: vegan, GMO-free soy dog. It may be "Not," but it's still "Hot."

MADE IN BROOKLYN

mibpizza.com

Instagram @madeinbrooklynnypizza

People from New York City *love* to tell you that they're from New York City and that nothing anybody does food-wise outside of the Big Apple can compare to what's happening in their hometown. Especially pizza. Luckily, the pizza at Made in Brooklyn is so damn good, as well as authentically East Coast-ish, that it satisfies even the most-dyed-in-the-wool Gothamite.

The slices are of that long, triangular, foldable style, with a crisp crust, served on the traditional white paper plate. My routine is to get a pair of cheese slices and a soda, then complain—in my really bad fake Bronx accent—loudly and ad nauseam about how Giuliani ruined Times Square. Goes over gangbusters, especially with people who were born after that happened and have no idea what I'm talking about.

The stromboli is great as well, and as big as a house. You can also call ahead and order a whole pie. I have this place on speed dial.

DAVE'S HOT CHICKEN

Instagram @daveshotchicken

Less a truck and more a pop-up Nashville hot chicken revival, Dave's Hot Chicken operates out of a parking lot in the heart of Thai Town. Run by a small crew hell-bent on delivering blazin' hot fowl, the seating is sparse (a couple of long tables and chairs), and the line can be long, but the heat is worth the wait.

The usual order is the chicken tenders in one of three sauces (mild,

Dave's Hot Chicken

medium, or hot), served with kale slaw and fries on top of a slice of white bread. I go with the "hot" sauce because I like to show my taste buds who's in charge. The kale slaw is supremely good: creamy and textured, it helps balance the heat. It's the next best thing to being in Music City.

AVE 26 TACO STAND

W Ave 26 and Humboldt St

Ave 26 brings a community together—literally. This place is packed most nights of the week, and for good reason: the tacos here are top-notch. This is not really a truck, but a legit, old-school taco stand. There's no seating—that's what your car is for. But what they do have

is some of the best al pastor tacos around. Load up on the grilled onions they offer as well as the chunks of diced potatoes stewing in boiling stomach fat. Yum yum!

BABY'S BADASS BURGERS

babysbadassburgers.com

Instagram @babysbbs

The brainchild of ex-New Yorker restaurateur Erica Cohen, noted events planner Lori Barbera, and Executive Chef Jason Ryczek, Baby's Badass Burgers' hot pink truck can be seen all around the city, dishing out some truly, uh, badass burgers, baby! The Original Beauty is just that, with Swiss cheese, grilled onions, sautéed mushrooms, and something called Baby's special sauce. It is juicy beyond belief. Sidecar that biz with some curly fries, which they call Pig Tails. Adorable.

For the hungry baby, try "The Bombshell." This ½-pound "Maneater" is sandwiched between two slices of bacon and grilled cheese melts, and topped with grilled onions and, of course, Baby's sauce.

 ## BELLY BOMBZ

bellybombz.com

Instagram @bellybombz

Chef and owner Albert Shim started Belly Bombz as a food stand at a local Long Beach farmers' market back in 2012. It has since grown to a brick-and-mortar location, and, of course, the hit food wagon seen everywhere from Beverly Hills to Hermosa Beach. BB is a mixture of Shim's Korean roots and his training in classical French cuisine—and what comes out is some bomb-ass chicken tenders and wings.

My fave is the Firecracker tenders, which is sweet and spicy traditional Korean fried chicken. The sauce is the star here. You can even take a bottle of it home with you. I put it on everything—especially my new Polo button down. Couple these birds with either the Miso Citrus Slaw or the Steamed Jasmine Rice. For you non-meat-eaters, you can substitute the ultra-tasty Pork Belly sliders for the equally tasty Crispy Tofu. Bombz away!

BEST PLACES TO EAT AT LAX

For that nine-hour flight delay.

10. LA Provence (T6)

9. Grilled Cheese Please! (T5)

8. The Habit (T6)

7. Border Grill (Tom Bradley International)

6. Ford's Filling Station (T5)

5. Reilly's Irish Pub (T1)

4. Ink.Sack (TBI)

3. Cole's (T4)

2. James' Beach (TBI)

1. Osteria (T6)

RAGIN' CAJUN TRUCK

ragincajun.com/cajun-on-wheels

Twitter @cajunonwheels

The Ragin' Cajun truck serves up pure, authentic Bayou Country cuisine, which means most of the menu is round, brown, and mighty good. Mostly operating in the South Bay of LA, as well as Burbank, this is the place to find some of the best fried catfish po'boys west of Bourbon Street.

A specialty of this truck is the different Bayou Bowls: basically a bowl of rice and red beans served with either chicken or sausage gumbo. And don't you dare pass up on the dessert. For only $5, they have a cheesecake with praline sauce that will bring a flood of joy to your taste receptors.

THE SURFER TACO

thesurfertaco.com

Twitter @thesurfertaco

Duuuude. If you're looking for some chill vibes, cool peeps, and some gnarly fish and shrimp tacos, then this landlocked tribute to beach culture is nirvana. I like to hit this place up after a few sun-drenched hours of hula-hooping and boogie boarding . . . OK, I'll level with you—I've never set foot in the ocean and I rarely go to the beach.

Anyway, just because I hate the ocean doesn't mean I can't enjoy the delicacies it has to offer. Like a big hearty Lobster Burrito filled with rice, beans, pico de gallo, cheese, cabbage, and Surfer Taco's secret dude sauce. It's not actually called dude sauce. But it should be.

THE GARBAGE TRUCK

garbagetruckfoodtruck.com

Instagram @thegarbagetruck

While it might not be the most appetizing name for a mobile eatery, not to mention the ungainly domain name, the Garbage Truck does serve

one hell of a Trash Plate. Apparently a "trash plate" is common grub to Upstate New Yorkers. You start with macaroni salad, add a generous helping of crisp and golden-brown home fries, slap on two cheeseburger patties, and dump a ladle's worth of hot meat sauce on it all. Finish it off with drizzles of mustard and ketchup and top it with chopped onions and you've got what could apparently only be named a Trash Plate.

It's not pretty but it is kind of delicious. If it seems a bridge too far for your appetite, they also serve pizza "logs" that are phenomenal too. Like something you and your college roomie tossed in the oven after the bars closed, a pizza log is pepperoni and cheese in a wonton wrapper. They also have hot dog logs. As you'd expect.

 ### INDIA JONES CHOW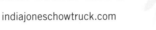

indiajoneschowtruck.com

Twitter @indiajonesCT

Chef Sumant Pardal comes from a long line of Indian restaurateurs, even running the East India Grill in LA. Now, with India Jones Chow truck, he is best known for serving up a roti, which is basically an Indian burrito. Filled with lamb, paneer, and mushrooms, this is an aromatic treat.

However, the Butter Chicken Curry—a rich and creamy dish that goes best with their Garlic Naan for dippin'—is most likely to get me reaching for my gold-plated money clip. This truck is mainly found in Santa Monica. So Eastsiders, you must head west for a taste of the Far East. Ironic!

 ### COUSINS MAINE LOBSTER

cousinsmainelobster.com

Instagram @cousinsmainelobster

Fun fact: Lobster wasn't always seen as the high-priced delicacy it is today. On ships carrying prisoners, the inmates were fed these clawed crustaceans. As punishment.

Well, we now know better. Lobster is usually reserved for dinners celebrating graduations, closing that big account, and winning a Tony. Not to mention the annual national observance of Lobsterfest.

Surely lobster is too highfalutin for a food truck? Nope. Say hello to Cousins Maine Lobster truck. Started by actual cousins in 2012, after appearing on the hit show *Shark Tank*, the Cousins Maine Lobster truck uses only the freshest caught lobsters for their menu. And what a menu! You can get the standard Maine Lobster Roll, served chilled with a New England-style roll. But we're not here to be standard. And don't forget that this is LA, where fusion is everything. I recommend the Lobster Quesadilla. Maine lobster, cheese, pico de gallo, and cilantro lime sauce on handmade flour tortillas. It's wicked awesome, *ese*.

THE CARNIVAL TRUCK

thecateringcarnival.com

Instagram @carnivaltruckla

So, it's come to this. I've told you all about the trucks that serve the best tacos, the most juicy burgers, and the snappiest hot dogs, but we end this section with a truck that will capture not only your taste buds, but your childlike sense of wonder. Behold! The Carnival Truck. Yes, people, a truck that serves "gourmet" carnival food.

Lest you forget which country we live in, this truck serves up the finest of fried finger foods, such as deep-fried mushrooms and mini corn dogs! You also, by law, have to try the Fritos Walkin' Taco. Choice of meat with sour cream, cheese, and cilantro. If that sounds too healthy for you, then go straight to the dessert section, pal. Everything here gets dunked into the fry-a-lator! Oreos! Twinkies! Brownie Bites! And don't forget the Miniature Cinnamon Rolls! Each topped with powdered sugar and drizzled with chocolate sauce. Best part of this truck? No clowns anywhere in sight. Clowns scare the heck out of me.

ACKNOWLEDGMENTS

This book would not have been written without the inspiration and support of Angel Johnston. Thanks also to everyone at The Countryman Press, especially Ann Treistman, and to Róisín Cameron for her editorial guidance. Thanks to James Greer, for his friendship above all else. Thanks to Tad Floridis—hope I didn't mess this up. Finally, a general thanks to everyone who works in the service industry, from the front of the house to the back. So many of you bust your ass to feed total strangers. This book is for you.

BEST BY NEIGHBORHOOD

ARLINGTON HEIGHTS

Olympic Cafe House of Breakfast 43

ARTS DISTRICT

Arts District Brewing 117

Bestia 130

Everson Royce Bar 84

Guerilla Tacos 70

Pearl's BBQ 94

Pizzanista! 86

Wurstküche 179

ATWATER VILLAGE

Proof Bakery 55

Tacos Villa Corona 26

The Village Bakery and Cafe 72

Wanderlust Creamery 163

BEVERLY GROVE

A.O.C 125

Joan's on Third 67

BEVERLY HILLS

Il Tramezzino 173

Maude 132

Sotto 151

Spago 122

BRENTWOOD

Baltaire 49

Bottlefish 51

Pizzana 89

BURBANK

Bob's Big Boy 165

Porto's Bakery & Cafe 55

CHINATOWN

Burgerlords 83

Howlin' Rays 68

Little Jewel of New Orleans 69

Nick's Cafe 27

CULVER CITY OOO

A-Frame 45

Blind Barber 103

The Corner Door 165

Johnnie's Pastrami 169

S + W Country Diner 38

Tentenyu 177

DTLA

71Above 142

Astro Doughnuts & Fried Chicken 51

Bäco Mercat 74

Badmaash 49

Birdies 161

Birds & Bees 103

Boomtown Brewery 117

Brack Shop Tavern 116

Bread Lounge 55

G & B 23

Maru Coffee 23

Meatzilla! 58

Modern Times 117

Nick + Stef's Steakhouse 100

ABOUT THE AUTHOR

MIKE POSTALAKIS is a writer and comedian based in Los Angeles. His comedy sketches and music videos have been featured on numerous websites including *Funny or Die*, *Pitchfork*, *AV Club*, and *USA Today*. Since moving to a thriving culinary metropolis such as Los Angeles, Mike has developed a keen interest (some would say an obsession) with finding the perfect breakfast burrito.